TO ALBERT SCHWEITZER

To

Dr. ALBERT

A Festschrift

From A Few

JANUARY 14, 1955, EVANSTON, ILLINOIS

SCHWEITZER

Commemorating His 80th Birthday

Of His Friends

FRIENDS OF ALBERT SCHWEITZER

CONTENTS

Salutations

DR. SCHWEITZER'S
ONE ANSWER
TO THE PROBLEM
OF THE MANY

▶

by J. S. BIXLER

LIFE makes many demands on all of us and most of us respond with personalities that are divided in greater or lesser degrees. Dr. Schweitzer, however, is notable for the unity he has been able to win without sacrificing the richness experience offers or failing to take account of its variety. Indeed it is the diversity of his interests that to many people is the most conspicuous thing about him. The many-sidedness of his intellectual life, his versatility as metaphysician, musician, and man of medicine and his ability to fuse these interests in his work as a missionary is well known. Further, he is not only a many-sided scholar but a scholar in action and his status as one of our generation's outstanding leaders derives in part from this fact.

But the diversity in unity that I should like to discuss here goes deeper. It shows in his alternating appeals to reason and to feeling, in his successive moods of despair and confidence, and perhaps most clearly in his ability at the same time to be a doubter and a man of faith.

The difference between reason and feeling as guides to the basic presuppositions of experience seems to haunt Dr.

Schweitzer and to influence all his work. *Weltanschauung* or world-view is what he calls the result of rational thought, *Lebensanschauung* or life-view the contribution of feeling and intuition. Dr. Schweitzer turns to each with such eagerness and such loyal willingness to respond that we wonder how the two conflicting claims can ever be reconciled. We must think for ourselves, he tells us. We must be utterly devoted to the truth. We must resist the tendency to dumb submissiveness before the assaults of propaganda and we must be on the alert against the unworthy suggestion that in this age of specialized knowledge we should rely on the thought of others. Standing out against a strong contemporary prejudice that would belittle the eighteenth century Dr. Schweitzer keeps insisting that the age of reason had special virtues that we should make our own. Many of his pages sound as if written by a person convinced that logic, proof, and the methods of rationalism offered the final keys to salvation for this or any other time.

And yet—on other pages Dr. Schweitzer tells us of the "crushing" effects of knowledge, the blind alleys of the intellect, and of the need for mystical insight if the ultimate answers are to be ours. It is a striking fact also that his own use of intellectual procedures varies and with it his own idea of their relevance to our deepest problems and of the significance of reason itself for life seems to change. At times he turns with apparent whole-heartedness to historical research. Yet is it not fair to say that when he comes to the person of Jesus he acts as if historical fact were of little account? It is universal truths that we are concerned with when Jesus speaks and it is noteworthy that their validity does not depend on the truths historical research brings to light. A different kind of intellectual method and another type of appraisal is brought into play when we enter the realm of metaphysics. And yet history retains its own kind of importance. Even within the realm of thought conflicting claims appear that must be reconciled.

Another interesting example of apparently divided loyalties is found in Dr. Schweitzer's approach to music and particularly in his idea of what a composer like Bach has to say to us. Both in the introduction to the Widor-Schweitzer edition of Bach's works and in his life of the great polyphonist, Dr. Schweitzer frequently treats Bach as a rationalist in the sense of one whose power comes from his grasp of closely-knit, well-articulated and coherent form. We must submit to Bach as to an objective standard that has its own type of rational correctness, relegating our own subjective preferences to a subordinate place. Yet was not Dr. Schweitzer also one of the first to point out the pictorial quality in Bach's work and the immediacy of its appeal to our emotions?

The division between heart and head comes out poignantly in Dr. Schweitzer's varying moods of optimism and pessimism. He must be essentially an optimist, we feel, or he could never have accomplished what he has. Yet he tells us that often he is a pessimist. "Only at quite rare moments," he says, "have I felt really glad to be alive." Significantly, and somewhat surprisingly for one who sets so much store by the intellect, he points out that knowledge is bound to be pessimistic and that optimism rests on the feelings and the will. The head, so necessary, so apparently dependable, so consistent, defeats its own purposes. The heart, so unstable, so quick and so fickle, is ultimately our support and stay.

I think readers of Dr. Schweitzer also fail at times to see his combination of rigorous and assured faith with equally rigorous and devastating doubt. Where can we find a religious leader who has been so honest in expressing his skepticism? And how much religion has lost, one cannot help adding,

5

just because its apologists have been so slow to recognize doubt's positive qualities. One of the clearest evidences of Dr. Schweitzer's greatness, not only as thinker but as man of faith, seems to me to be his readiness to bring honest questionings out into the open and to recognize their positive significance. To be skeptically critical is to use our powers of analysis in response to a moral ideal and the fact that we use these powers at all means that we are sensitive to the ideal and its claim. Dr. Schweitzer calls this fact forcefully to our attention.

Indeed no one could be more explicit about it. Where are the evidences for this God?—he asks us at times. I find not one increasing purpose, he remarks, but cross-currents that interfere with and frustrate one another. Nature, where God should be, remains an enigma. God does not seem to exist in his world. At least our knowledge cannot find him. And if knowledge is helpless, where can we turn? Here, as so often, Dr. Schweitzer seems both to affirm and deny and yet we cannot help feeling that the denial is in its way a re-affirmation. The denial points beyond itself and the affirmation is not so much undercut as caught up into a new kind of positiveness.

The easiest way to see what this means is, I think, to observe first of all that Dr. Schweitzer gives us his own modern variant of the ancient theme that the seeker finds what he looks for not in a specific answer to his question but in a new understanding of what is implied in the conditions of the search. In history and literature alike the honest questioner who has brought both persistency and imagination to his task has found his goal even though it was not what he thought it was going to be. This has been true of such different historical characters as Socrates and William James just as it has of poetic figures like Job and Faust. For each a discovery of the conditions of the quest brought its own conviction of the rightness of the quest itself and of the creative forces that provided for it.

To this age-old situation Dr. Schweitzer adds a new touch. What impels us to make the search?—he asks in effect. Why should we torture ourselves over such questions? Indeed, why should we not only think and suffer but why should we live at all when to live means to be buffeted about by so many winds of doctrine?

As is well known, Dr. Schweitzer appeals here to his basic affirmation—I am life that wills to live in the midst of other life that wills to live. Do we always notice the significance of this appeal? Do we see, in the first place, that Dr. Schweitzer reaches it only after traversing the entire path of doubt? I may doubt all else, including the outside world and all my impressions of it, but I cannot doubt my own inner life. I cannot question the feelings that lie at the springs of my will to live and even my will to doubt itself. The will to live is indubitable. But it is very significant that Dr. Schweitzer goes further than this. To stop here would be to remain with Nietzsche who also proclaimed the will to live and it would have meant going on with Nietzsche to affirm the will to power. Instead, Dr. Schweitzer recognizes his will to live as one in the midst of other wills to live and thus as leading not to the will to power but the will to love. My awareness of my own will, that is to say, is itself an awareness of a larger will that works through me and I am led inevitably to an awareness of other wills with a dignity similar to mine and an irresistible claim on my attention.

Now let us be sure we see what is involved here. Dr. Schweitzer has taken us back to the bedrock of certainty in showing us the datum that cannot be doubted. But he has gone on to point out that this datum of the emotions, this intuitive awareness of the will to live, leads us on to the re-employment of the methods of the intellect that we thought we had discarded. For what is this awareness of other wills than my own but a new appeal to the methods of the head? What does the scientist do but take his initial datum and relate it to other relevant data? What is the aim of the intellect but that of discovering not merely facts but relationships among facts? Dr. Schweitzer has turned in disillusionment from the head to the ultimate insights of the heart, but has found that they make use of the head's methods and require the restoration of the purposes and processes of the mind to their place of partnership.

This is suggestive, I think, of the real synthesis that Dr. Schweitzer offers us. Where others see disunity and even conflict, Dr. Schweitzer, without minimizing real differences, finds a basic harmony. Conspicuous as he is for the diversity of his interests, his life is yet more noteworthy for the working consistency it has been able to achieve. In his hands not only have head and heart joined forces but the many have become one without losing their colorfulness or the richness of their individual appeal.

A final illustration from nineteenth century European philosophy may help to show how successfully Dr. Schweitzer brings together the two separate and sometimes conflicting appeals of reason and emotion. When Dr. Schweitzer was a student, philosophy was torn by the competing claims of Kantian idealism on the one hand and Nietzschean dynamism or vitalism on the other. For the idealist, mind is supreme and an object has reality only as it is itself mind or is related to it as idea. For the vitalist, on the other hand, mind is a kind of secondary or even retrogressive factor that impedes the full exercise of the dramatic, imperious instincts the life force places at our disposal. Now Dr. Schweitzer, like the rest of us, has his existence on the plane of life, so to say, that is as a person governed by the purposes, ambitions, and drives which are the sign of life working in us. Yet he has explicitly shown how as a person he governs his desires and purposes by making them submit to the claims resident in abstract ideas. Notice the Platonic triad of abstractions he sets before us. He tells us above all else to seek the truth, and even in his most "religious" books he refuses to allow any supposedly religious or higher claim to supersede that of accurate consistency. When he plays Bach he again submits his personal tastes to the objective standards that governed Bach's own sense for abstract form. And when one asks Dr. Schweitzer why he went to Africa he replies very simply that he did it in the name of justice and as his own attempt to pay some part of the debt the white man had owed his black brother for so long. Truth, beauty, and justice have been Dr. Schweitzer's guides. As a living man with instinctive desires he has reached out to abstract ideas for help and has found in their formal consistency what he needed for the regulation of his own life.

But notice that this is not all. As a philosopher, thinking about ideas, communing with them, and absorbing what they have to offer, he reaches back once more to the plane on which dynamic vital impulse furnishes the answer. For is not the key conception of his philosophy "reverence for life"? Is not this the base on which his structure of ethical theory is raised? As a practical man looking for ways out of practical dilemmas, Dr. Schweitzer turns to abstract ideas. And as a philosopher, seeking the answer to questions of theory, he returns to the datum vouchsafed by our feelings. Here indeed is a productive synthesis which refuses to assign to either word or deed the place of honor on the day of creation but insists that both are joined in a cooperative partnership.

The fact that Dr. Schweitzer goes on to show that their unity is for him not merely a matter of theory but a means to constructive achievement is what makes his testimony so eloquent, so memorable, and so impossible to deny.

J. S. Bixler

JULIUS SEELYE BIXLER was born in New London, Connecticut, in 1894 He was educated at Amherst College and Yale University He has been invited to deliver lectures to many foundations, and some of these have been published as *Immortality and the Present World* (Ingersoll Lectures in 1931), *Religion for Free Minds* (Lowell Lectures in 1939), and *Conversations with an Unrepentant Liberal* (Terry Lecture in 1951) Since 1942 he has been president of Colby College in Waterville, Maine In the late twenties he visited Dr Schweitzer in Germany to invite him to deliver the Lowell Lectures in Boston He has been chairman of the Albert Schweitzer Fellowship.

A REALIST OF THE SPIRIT

▶

by MARTIN BUBER

WHEN I heard in 1905 that the Privatdozent in Theology, Albert Schweitzer, had begun to study medicine, I noticed it with interest, and when I heard eight years later that he had gone to the Congo not as a missionary but as a doctor in order to fight a serious sickness with which the natives were afflicted, the event assumed for me a positively symbolical character. I had become acquainted with Schweitzer in 1901 or 1902 through an essay of his on the mystery of the Last Supper. This essay made a deep impression on me because it brought Jesus into close relation with the mysteries of Jewish faith. Already at that time I called Schweitzer a theological realist because he saw the manifestations of the spirit in the context of the particular realities of faith in which they made their appearance. Now, with his study of medicine and his emigration to Lambaréné, he proved by his own life that he was a realist of the spirit. To the realists whom I mean, men are not so fundamentally divided into body and soul that when one wishes to help them, one may give one's attention exclusively to the soul. Where one is met by widespread bodily suffering to whose healing one believes oneself able to make an essential contribution, one feels oneself called to this task. The true doctor indeed has to do with body and soul in one, but the bodily suffering is manifest and it is with it that he must begin, though not without giving the soul a share in the process. If one approaches a doctor such as this, a man who is, to begin with, a theologian and who is destined to remain a theologian as long as he lives, and asks: "Must you not first of all concern yourself with the soul?" he answers: "The soul knows better how to wait than the body." and in saying this he remained, in fact, in the following of his master, who certainly did not begin again and again with the healing of bodily infirmities merely in order to give a sign.

Such was the manner of Schweitzer's working in the sphere of the participation of the spirit of life. But also in the sphere of spiritual work itself he remains the realist. His theological research has always been centrally concerned with the understanding of primitive Christianity as closely allied with the believing man's will toward the salvation of the world and the believing man's interpretation of the contemporary age as the aeon of salvation that has already begun. The spiritualized conception of redemption thus regained for Schweitzer its basic meaning, that of the factual salvation on earth of the whole human being.

But bound up with all this in addition is Schweitzer's philosophy, whose leading idea is reverence for human life. This concept refers us once more to the body-soul totality of the individual living man as that which is to be actively honored and helped. Not only ethical but also political questions will be misunderstood if one thinks that one may deal with them as independent of the awesome reality of human living and dying.

Schweitzer's relation, as scholar and interpreter, to Bach, the great realist of the believing spirit, is also to be understood in its essence from this standpoint.

To us, before whose eyes spirit and life have fallen apart from each other more radically perhaps than in any earlier time, it is a great comfort and encouragement that this man exists, in whom their created togetherness is manifested and confirmed.

(This essay has been translated from the German by Dr. Maurice S. Friedman of Bronxville, New York.)

MARTIN BUBER was born in Vienna, Austria, in 1878. He was educated at universities in Vienna, Berlin, Leipzig, and Zurich. He was Professor of Comparative Religion at the University of Frankfurt from 1923-33 He is the author of many volumes on Hasidism and Zionism, including *I and Thou* (1937) and *Hasidism* (1948). Since 1938 he has been Professor of Social Philosophy at the Hebrew University in Jerusalem, Israel.

THE BELIEF OF
SCHWEITZER
IN THE POWER
OF THE SPIRIT

▶

by FRITZ BURI

IN his Goethe address given in Aspen, Colorado, Schweitzer explains that the greatness of the *Weltanschauung* of Goethe lies in two points. The first point is that, as the great idealists of his time, Goethe understands man as that being in which the spirit will triumph over nature. The second point is that he—in contrast to Kant, Fichte, Schelling, and Hegel—has refused to construct from this Spirit-principle, through epistemological or speculative manipulations, a universal *Weltanschauung*, out of which Ethics should be derived. This basic thought, which is Schweitzer's own *Weltanschauung*, along with many other points, links him with Goethe, and he develops this thought again and again in his ethical, theological, and biographical writings. The philosophical expression of this principle is that, although the dualistic systems do not correspond to the universal desire of the spirit, they are ethically more valuable than the monistic systems because the latter do mistake the enigma of the ethical moment. Expressed in the terms of Christian theology: the Christ-mysticism of Paul is to be preferred to the God-mysticism of John. And once again the same thing is in a picture from the world of Schweitzer: it does not succeed to the doctrine, Reverence for Life, to make out of itself an all-embracing Cathedral. It contents itself with the erection of a choir-place. But therein it worships God without interruption.

Let us then clarify this somewhat in detail, and by contrasting this conception of Schweitzer's, which he has found in Goethe, to variant conceptions of our time.

As at all times, there is also today an idealism which is persuaded that in man and through man the Spirit is destined to conquer nature in the world. To be a man does not mean simply to give full rein to one's natural desires, but to seek after the purpose of life and to attempt to realize it. Schweitzer defines this purpose in an elementary and comprehensive way as Reverence for Life; i.e., an attitude determined by the natural will of life, deepened by thought, which—as such—must esteem not only its own life but all life; which must consider all damage to life as guilt; and which must seize every opportunity to further life as an opportunity of atonement. Therein lies, as Schweitzer has shown, the essence of real culture.

However, man would like to have a guarantee that that spirit will finally triumph. He desires this guarantee because he sees in himself and around himself powers quite different from this idea of culture, namely, the sheer will to live and wildly destructive natural powers. And so man constructs for himself—in religious, mythological pictures, or in politico-social Utopias, or in philosophical speculations—a perfect world, a coming kingdom of God, a future paradise on earth in a classless society, or in a pure spirit-world for which the material is only an illusion.

But there can follow an adjustment to nature of these ideals which should lead man beyond nature and the result is a mere utilitarian, moral—or even a demonical—justification of immoral acts of violence and institutions for the sake of a so-called higher or even holy purpose. A second possibility is that the optimism about the future asserts itself in the face of all hindrances and believes blindly and stubbornly in the miracle. Then, when the miracle does not appear, but the sense-enigma of the world inexorably reveals itself, this optimism falls into a completely abysmal despair about God and man and all good. We have for this occurrence plenty of examples in our time.

We live today definitely in a world filled with the ruins of religious and philosophical, political and economic ideologies. We hit each other on the head with the broken fragments of such ideologies. Possessed by anxiety, we seek to secure ourselves behind iron curtains. We are in the danger of declining to the level of a cave-man, to an existence which is able to expel all nature-enthusiasm. Neither stock-exchange nor altars, neither parties nor hierarchies, will be able to stop this decline.

Let us hear now in this apocalypse of nihilism the truly prophetic voice of Albert Schweitzer. He has foreseen this catastrophe. He has recognized that our civilization has no longer been guided by spirit, but that we have become the slaves of our inventions, and that we could deceive ourselves regarding this situation through outward success and thoughtlessness. That which has taken place in the world since the beginning of his studies about Culture-Philosophy has only confirmed his pessimistic prognosis, but it has not been able to break his optimism, because his optimism is not a superficial kind, but is a truly believing one, founded in ethical thinking.

The principal meaning of Schweitzer's Culture-Philosophy for our despairing time is that he shows us the way to a genuine, active optimism. He gives us two basic directions:

First is thinking precisely, elementary and consistent thinking. Schweitzer is a rationalist and does not hesitate to confess himself a rationalist even in this age, which almost despairs of thinking and is ready to throw itself into the arms of all kinds of irrationalism. According to Schweitzer, the special potentiality and dignity of man lies in thinking. Apart from thinking, man becomes the victim of dark powers and forces and sinks to the bare natural state. However, it may not be an artificial, unreal thinking, but it must be an elementary, comprehensible, and therefore cogent thinking—a thinking which does not move in thin abstractions, but grows out of the realities of concrete life and proves its rightness by repeated application in concrete life. This thinking proves its power in that, when it deals with reality, it does not violate reality or misinterpret it, but it remains true to its acquired perception, and thus becomes the motive and idea of formative action. Schweitzer has for this a formula: Reverence for Life—"I am life which wills to live, in the midst of life which wills to live."

Second is elementary and ethical thinking which must be at once humble and high-minded. It may not believe itself able to construct all of the universe according to its ideas. We do not sit in the council of the gods. And life is deeper than we mortals like to think. Not only nature, but—much more—history, is full of abstruse riddles. We do not know why life can live only at the cost of other life, why there is meaninglessness and evil in the world. The greatness of the ethical thinking of Schweitzer lies in the fact that it dares to be, in this relation, agnostic and that it does not postulate a history of salvation, or a spirit-world with the help of religious or philosophical speculations, but that it remains humble before the inexplicable riddle. But in this very attitude, it becomes a real high-mindedness in that it perceives itself to be the light in the darkness, the special sense-possibility of man in the midst of the sense-mystery of the world. Where it becomes possible for us to think and to act out of Reverence for Life, there the darkness lightens itself a little, there appears sense and there sense can be realized. And when one, to whom this possibility appears, recognizes this possibility as a gift, a grace of God, thus at the same time he will become aware of himself as chosen by God as a place and instrument of the redemption of God. Schelling's idea of the evolving God is here to be noticed. But Schweitzer prefers here—quite rightly—the original conception of Christ: Christ as a symbol for a special, saving, creative power of God. Therefore he declares the apostle Paul to be the great Christian thinker because the apostle has found in his Christ-mysticism the permanent, symbolic expression of this sense-possibility of human existence. Paul does not say as John, that God is love, but that we become one with God through love in the spirit of Christ. We cannot exhaust the depths of this God, but it is not necessary to attempt it. It is sufficient for us that he reveals himself in our loving as the lover.

Let us now see what practical consequences Schweitzer develops out of the above-discussed principles in his Culture-Philosophy and let us choose two viewpoints especially important for our time.

Also here can we take for a starting-point the spiritual kinship of Schweitzer with Goethe. It is always revealing for the character of a man to see what he emphasizes in another person and what he considers to be exemplary.

First, Schweitzer admires in Goethe above all his struggle for pure humanity, both in the way in which Goethe struggles with his own nature and in the way in which he brings this ideal to expression in the characters of his works. And here is to be mentioned above all the figure of Iphigenia, which has powerfully attracted Schweitzer. As Iphigenia, rejecting force and deceit and trusting only in strength of truth, dares to confront the dark tyrant, Thoas, Goethe sees in her the incarnation of purest humanity. One may protest that the conversion of Thoas is psychologically improbable. However, Goethe brings to expression thereby his belief in the power of truth. Going beyond Goethe's idealism, Schweitzer's thought allies us with truth, although we have no theoretical or practical guarantee that truth will triumph. To renounce truth because of this danger of defeat would mean in any case to betray the spirit to force.

I must not fail at this point to quote to you some sentences which Schweitzer has written about the power of the ideal in his book, *Memoirs of Childhood and Youth*: "We must all be prepared to find that life tries to take from us our belief in the good and the true, and our enthusiasm for them, but we need not surrender them. That ideals, when they are brought into contact with reality, are usually crushed by facts does not mean that they are bound from the very beginning to capitulate to the facts, but merely that our ideals are not strong enough; and they are not strong enough because they are not pure and strong and stable enough in ourselves. The power of ideals is incalculable. We see no power in a drop of water. But let it get into a crack in the rock and be turned to ice, and it splits the rock; turned into steam, it drives the pistons of the most powerful engines. Something has happened to it which makes active and effective the power that is latent in it. So it is with ideals. Ideals are thoughts. So long as they exist merely as thoughts, the power latent in them remains ineffective, however great the enthusiasm, and however strong the conviction with which the thought is held. Their power only becomes effective when they are taken up into some refined human personality."

Thus is Schweitzer a realist—but a realist of the spirit.

And he is a realist in that his trust in the power of the spirit does not mean a false optimism before evil. His realism shows itself, for instance, in his very realistic pronouncements on colonial questions. Out of his own acquaintance with colored people, he knows that one does them no favor when one, for example, allows them democratic liberties for whose use they are by no means ready and which bring them only into temptation to abuse these liberties. Thus when a native in his hospital carries out a task only desultorily, Schweitzer holds himself responsible because he has failed to exert the necessary control. Through his too great a trust, he has brought them into temptation to give themselves over to their propensities, in this case to laziness. With all our trusting in the power of the spirit, we must not give an opponent the temptation to interpret our idealism as weakness; otherwise we invite him to use force. We must take care that he lets well enough alone.

The second point which Schweitzer has likewise in common with Goethe, and which belongs also to our theme, concerns the attitude toward modern technology and organization. As minister to his prince, Goethe lived not all of the time for his poetry and other spiritual things, but he occupied himself very much and with all his energy with very sober and prosaic things, for instance, with street improvements and social tasks. And as a passionate scientist, which he was, he employed a great amount of time for all kinds of experiments, particularly in connection with his theory of colors and the metamorphosis of plants. But thereby he was, as Schweitzer emphasizes, very hesitant in the use of technical helps. And when he felt it necessary, he could give his time and attention quite freely to a single person.

To illustrate this last characteristic of Goethe, Schweitzer mentioned in an earlier speech about Goethe, the journey into the Harz mountains which he once took in the cold and fog in order to comfort a young man, who found himself in spiritual difficulty. And thereby Schweitzer remarks that, since then, whenever he must make a sacrifice of time and strength in order to serve a brother who needs his help, he is accustomed to remember Goethe and to say to himself, "This is now my journey into the Harz."

Thus Schweitzer heard the call of the mission to help the natives of the Congo area, who needed the ministry of a physician, and at thirty years of age he began to study medicine and founded afterwards his hospital for Negroes, for which he has sacrificed already so very many other and—to us—apparently important plans. So Lambaréné became his great "journey into the Harz" which even now every hour fully occupies the eighty-year-old Schweitzer. However, through Lambaréné, more than through all of his scientific and artistic works, has Schweitzer's name become a symbol for all mankind, a symbol of the direct service of the individual, in which—as hardly anywhere else in this time of the masses and of force—the triumphant power of the spirit has become a comforting and inspiring reality. In his writings, Schweitzer has repeatedly used this attitude represented by him as the basis of a genuine culture. With astute analysis, he shows in his Culture-Philosophy that true progress is not based upon technology and organization, but that these, on the contrary, can become dangerous to progress if they are not guided by personal responsibility of the individual. This is not to say that Schweitzer is an enemy of inventions or a despiser of organization. Only the newest and best medicines and methods are good enough in his eyes for his hospital; tropical medicine has benefited from his experiments, and he is himself an extraordinary organizer. However, all who have been in Lambaréné testify that, without him, the hospital would not be what it is; he is the soul of it all, and even in the smallest details, the influence of his spirit is felt. As great and as worldwide as·his circle of helpers is, still the hospital is his own personal work.

Thus it is not out of mere theory, but out of very personal experience, that he writes about the so-called culture-progress: "Our civilization is doomed because it has developed with much greater vigor materially than it has spiritually. Its equilibrium has been destroyed . . . But in our enthusiasm for knowledge and power we have arrived at a mistaken conception of what civilization is. We overvalue the material gains wrung from nature, and have no longer present in our minds the true significance of the spiritual element in life . . . Through progress of knowledge and ability real culture is not made easier, but more difficult . . . The essence of culture does not consist of material achievements, but it lies in the fact that individuals have a vision of the perfection of man and of the improvement of social and political conditions of the nations and of mankind, and that the individuals are guided by such ideals in their thinking in a forceful and constant manner."

Concerning the problem of organization, however, we read this in Schweitzer's writings: "Our whole spiritual life nowadays has its course within organizations. From childhood up, the man of today has his mind so full of the thought of discipline that he loses the sense of his own individuality and can only see himself as thinking in the spirit of some group or other of his fellows . . . From year to year the thoughtless expansion of opinions by organizations becomes more and more developed. The methods of this expansion have arrived at such perfection and have found such an acceptance that the audacity to make the most absurd idea a legitimate, public opinion, when it seems to be profitable, does not need to be justified . . . The organized political, social and religious institutions of our time are attempting to bring the individual to the place where he will not acquire his opinions through his own thinking, but will accept these opinions as his own which these institutions offer him. A man, who thinks for himself and thereby is spiritually free, is for them something uncomfortable and frightening . . . The most purposeful improvements of the organization of our society, after which we must strive, can help us only when we are at the same time capable of giving our time a new spirit."

Therefore Schweitzer calls repeatedly for resistance against propaganda, against this cunning instrument of force, which turns the spirit into non-spirit: "A new public opinion must be created privately and unobtrusively. The existing one is maintained by the press, by propaganda, by organization, and by financial and other influences which are at its disposal. This unnatural way of spreading ideas must be opposed by the natural one, which goes from man to man and relies solely on the truth of the thoughts and the hearer's receptiveness for new truth. Unarmed and following the human spirit's primitive and natural fighting method, it must attack the other, which faces it, as Goliath faced David, in the mighty armor of the age . . ."

With this picture of David and Goliath, we shall close. We have here in gripping fashion symbolically summarized Albert Schweitzer's message to the question of spirit and force which here concerns us. Only out of the daring, self-sacrificing thinking, and acting of the individual, which respond when the need of the hour calls them forth, can we hope to overcome the Colossus of force, which threatens today freedom and human dignity. In a similar situation, David not only prayed and hoped for a miracle when he confronted Goliath, but he swung his sling and hit the mark with his stone. That was not Reverence for Life, but as Schweitzer explains in another context, it is an acting out of suprapersonal responsibility, which makes us guilty directly when we do our duty; and this experience is a revelation of our existence which is involved in the sense-riddle of history. Force does not become good because it may have a good purpose, but it remains evil. We well know this conflict today, and we may not avoid or even lessen this conflict, but we must think it through and endure it in all its violence. Thus only this conflict can bring us inner purification and the willingness to make atonement for unavoidable guilt. Just as no mere military victory can bring us this inward cleansing, just so can no outward defeat destroy it.

But all this — namely, responsibility and self-sacrifice, strength to incur guilt and to endure guilt, and the ability to consider the remaining span of our lives as an opportunity to make atonement for thoughtlessly acquired and unavoidable guilt—all these things which belong to a real humanity —Schweitzer has found in them what the New Testament means by the conception of Christ. And therefore his favorite text is the verse out of the Epistle to the Philippians: "And may the peace of God, which passeth all understanding, keep your hearts and minds in Christ Jesus."

F. Buri

FRITZ BURI was born in Berne, Switzerland, in 1907 He was educated at the universities of Basel, Berne, Marburg, and Berlin Since 1948 he has been minister of St. Alban in Basel and since 1951 he has been Professor of Systematic Theology at the University of Basel He is the author of many volumes, including *Christentum und Kultur bei Albert Schweitzer* (1941), *Albert Schweitzer und unser Zeit* (1947), *Albert Schweitzer und Karl Jaspers* (1950), and *Albert Schweitzer als Theologe heute* (1954). He is also the editor of *Festschrift fur Albert Schweitzer* (1955).

TO ALBERT SCHWEITZER

▶

by AMIYA CHAKRAVARTY

This is the great Tree, near the flowing Ogowe.
Mighty the root and power of the Tree, gentle its message
      from humanity.
Bearing shade and healing, resonant with deep voice from
      afar.
And mighty, and great is the Ogowe, the current of African
      life.

The far peoples, near to human heart, called dark
Because of our mind's nubian darkness, move:
This river Ogowe, inwardly burning, shines brighter in truth.
Transcending, in strength and agony, the tyranny of
      conquerors
The crucified continent awakes, is resurrected, unified
      each day.
And great is the Tree, with its message of reverence for all.
The current, the torrent of Ogowe, mingles with the murmur
      of leaves.

The Tree grows and deepens with the years, is beautiful,
Its words of peace, at last, in full defiance to war and horror
Are uttered now, while shadows gather in the horizon.
The living Tree fulfils itself, its courage of benediction grows.
And River Ogowe, the African river, also grows deep and full
And grows greater,

Till, at last, it reaches freedom, using freedom,
Drawing power, unafraid, from the eternal heart.
Unitive in its hard road of consecrated power,
Healing and fulfilling itself, ready to help the fallen
      conquerors
To redeem, and be redeemed, in equal mercy of God,
Using the great Tree's shade, and flowing beyond
      Lambaréné.

Amiya Chakravarty

AMIYA CHAKRAVARTY was born in West Bengal, India, in 1901. He graduated from Patna University and Oxford University He was associated both with Rabindranath Tagore and Mahatma Gandhi He was professor of English Literature and Humanities at Calcutta University from 1940-48 and official advisor to the Indian delegation at the United Nations, 1950-51 He is author of *The Dynasts and the Modern Age in Poetry* (1937) Since 1953 he has been Visiting Professor of Comparative Oriental Religions and Literature at Boston University. He visited Dr. Schweitzer several times in Europe.

AN ELEPHANT IN EBONY

▶

by DR. CLEMENT C. CHESTERMAN

"Prière d'accepter ce souvenir
Pensez à nous à l'avenir"

So spake the Demoiselle Mathilde,
Who with Miss Emma helped to build
The hospital at Lambaréné:
"This elephant, conceived in ebony
Will symbolize as best it can
Albert Schweitzer, Superman."

So spake she better than she knew
On the green verge of Ogowe,
Where the forest meets the water
Spake this brave Alsatian daughter.

Who but an elephant, I ask—
So elephantine was the task,
Could have trod so gently here
Where even angels well might fear?

Who else have strength to lift a log
Sunk in this vast primeval bog?
Who sense firm earth on which to stand
To elevate this Lazar's land?

Slow is the growth which brings to birth
The largest mammal on the earth,
And slow in the matrix of Alsace
Grew up a youth in truth and grace.

'Twas to the Vosges his eyes he'd raise
To fields, fir-edged where safely graze
Those sheep which Bach's rare melody
Kept ever in his memory.

To Olympian heights his mind aspired
To culture wide as Goethe's fired—
Not he to dream or walk on air,
But lay foundations firm, four-square.

The mysteries of Theology,
Great Music and Philosophy
If haply he the way might find
To God's most gracious ways and mind.

And finally the healing art
That he to man might show God's heart.
Thus, with a fourfold doctorate
To God his life was dedicate.

To the Unholy land he went,
Africa's mighty continent,
Foraging for his daily food
Challenging parasites' deadly brood.

Nor was crusader ever seen
With shield so strong or point so keen,
With such a tough integument,
Well to defend his argument.

Not he to trumpet his design,
But to a humble place resign
Himself among the common herd,
A life of service he preferred.

To heal the man, to bend the tree,
He set himself assiduously,
His massive shoulders mocked the weight
Of burdens whether small or great.

Instead of tusks a lance he used
To probe the flesh with germs infused;
A pen that, stronger than a sword,
Earned him the rare Nobel award.

No ivory tower were those points to him,
Or escape for indulgence of thought or whim,
But tools for unearthing the roots of disease
And weapons to fight any foe that he sees.

Unique versatility, strength without noise,
Spirituality, dignity, poise—
Life affirmation was his thought,
His life confirming what he taught.

Such is the doctor, rightly called great,
Whose eightieth year we celebrate—
Ere shades of the forest close round his head
Though he and his work will never be dead.

He blazed a trail to the Holy Grail,
Discovered it far from Communion rail,
The Life of God in the life for man
The Love of God in the love of man.

In reverence for Life, let His kingdom come,
Profoundest of truths in the simplest sum,
Let men rise up and work it out,
Follow his trail with a heart as stout.

Prenons nous tous ce beau souvenir,
Et gardons-le bien pour tout l'avenir.

CLEMENT C. CHESTERMAN was born in Bath, England,
in 1894 He was educated at the University of Bristol
and served as a physician in the Royal Army Medical
Corps. From 1920-36 he was a medical missionary with
the Baptist Missionary Society at Yakusu, Upper Bel-
gian Congo From 1936-49 he was medical officer and
secretary to the Baptist Missionary Society in London.
Since 1950 he has been in consulting practice in tropical medicine and teacher and examiner in tropical
medicine at the University of London. He is author of
Tropical Dispensary Handbook (1928) He is chairman
of the executive committee of the British Council of
the Dr. Schweitzer's Hospital Fund.

THE POINT ABOUT SCHWEITZER

▶

by NORMAN COUSINS

SOME travelers returning from brief visits to Dr. Schweitzer's hospital in French Equatorial Africa appear to be disillusioned. It seems that the good doctor hasn't been making use of all the modern medical facilities put at his disposal by friends in America and Europe. Also, it was observed that the mattresses in the hospital sickroom were without sheets. There are other complaints, all of them having to do with the fact that the hospital at Lambaréné isn't the most crisply scientific place in the world. Disenchantment has led these visitors to some open scoffing about the general capabilities of the humanitarian-physician-theologian-philosopher and about his right to world renown.

We haven't seen the mattresses at Dr. Schweitzer's African hospital, but even if every last one of them was split down the middle, with the beds teetering on three legs, we would still believe that Albert Schweitzer is one of the two or three greatest men to walk this earth in the past fifty years and that it is a privilege to be his contemporary. Nothing could be more absurd than to suggest that Dr. Schweitzer's reputation needs revision because his record in sanitation, such as there is of it, may be less than inspiring. When stuff such as this is used to diminish a truly towering figure the most charitable answer that can be given the belittlers is to say they have missed the point.

The point about Schweitzer is not whether he brought a gleaming modern hospital to Lambaréné. The point about Schweitzer is that he brought the kind of spirit to Africa that the dark man hardly knew existed in the white man. Before Schweitzer white skin meant beatings and gunpoint rule and the imposition of slavery on human flesh. If Schweitzer had done nothing else in his life than to accept the pain of these people as his own, he would have achieved eminence. And his place in history will rest on something more substantial than an argument over an unswept floor in a hospital ward in the heart of Africa. It will rest on the spotless nature of his vision and the clean sweep of his nobility.

The greatness of Schweitzer—indeed the essence of Schweitzer—is the man as symbol. It is not so much what he has done for others, but what others have done because of him and the power of his example. This is the measure of the man. What has come out of his life and thought is the kind of inspiration that can animate a generation. He has supplied a working demonstration of reverence for life. He represents enduring proof that we need not torment ourselves about the nature of human purpose. The scholar, he once wrote, must not live for science alone, nor the businessman for his business, nor the artist for his art. If affirmation for life is genuine, it will "demand from all that they should sacrifice a portion of their own lives for others."

Thus, Schweitzer's main achievement is a simple one. He has been willing to make the ultimate sacrifice for a moral principle. Like Gandhi, the power of his appeal has been in renunciation. And because he has been able to feel a supreme identification with other human beings he has exerted a greater force than millions of armed men on the march. It is unimportant whether we call Schweitzer a great religious figure or a great moral figure or a great philosopher. It suffices that his words and works are known and that he is loved and has influence because he enables men to discover mercy in themselves. Early in his life he was accused of being an escapist. He was criticized for seeming to patronize the people he had chosen to serve. Yet the proof of his genuineness and his integrity is to be found in the response he awakens in people. He has reached countless millions who have never seen him but who have been able to identify themselves with him because of the invisible and splendid fact of his own identification with them.

"I must forgive the lies directed against myself," he wrote, "because my own life has been so many times blotted by lies . . . I am obliged to exercise unlimited forgiveness because, if I did not, I should be untrue to myself, in that I should thus act as if I were not guilty in the same way as the other has been guilty with regard to me."

We live at a time when people seem afraid to be themselves, when they seem to prefer a hard, shiny exterior to the genuineness of deeply-felt emotion. Sophistication is prized and sentiment is dreaded. It is made to appear that one of the worst blights on a reputation is to be called a do-gooder. The literature of the day is remarkably devoid of themes on the natural goodness or even the potential goodness of man, seeing no dramatic power in the most powerful fact of the human mixture. The values of the time lean to a phony toughness, casual violence, cheap emotion; yet we are shocked when youngsters confess to having tortured and killed because they enjoyed it and because they thought it was the thing to do.

It matters not to Schweitzer or to history that he will be dismissed by some as a do-gooder or as a sentimental fool who fritters his life away on Africans who can't read or write. "Anyone who proposes to do good," he wrote, "must not expect people to roll stones out of his way, but must accept his lot calmly if they even roll a few more upon it." For the tragedy of life is not in the hurt to a man's name or even in the fact of death itself. The tragedy of life is in what dies inside a man while he lives—the death of genuine feeling, the death of inspired response, the death of the awareness that makes it possible to feel the pain or the glory of other men in oneself. Schweitzer's aim is not to dazzle an age but to awaken it, to make it comprehend that moral splendor is part of the gift of life, and that each man has unlimited strength to feel human oneness and to act upon it. He has proved that although a man may have no jurisdiction over the fact of his existence, he can hold supreme command over the meaning of existence for him. Thus, no man need fear death; he need fear only that he may die without having known his greatest power—the power of his free will to give his life for others.

If there is a need in America today, it is for a Schweitzer among us. We are swollen with meaningless satisfactions and dulled by petty immediacies—but the threat to this nation and its freedoms and to human life in general has never been greater. To the extent that part of this threat is recognized, it is assumed it can be adequately met by a posture of military and material strength. But the crisis is basically moral and demands moral strength.

We can't save the nation by acting as though only the nation is in jeopardy, or by acting as though the highest value is the nation. The highest value is the human being and the human potential. In order to safe-guard this human potential we have to do more than to surround ourselves with high explosives. We have to make the supreme identification with other people, including those who are different from us or who have less than we. If sacrifice is required, we shall have to sacrifice. If we are to lead, what we say and what we do must become more important in our own minds than what we sell or what we use. At a time when men possess the means for demolishing a planet the only business that makes sense is the business of inspired purpose.

Norman Cousins

NORMAN COUSINS was born in Union, New Jersey, in 1912. He was educated at Teachers College, Columbia University. He is the author of several volumes, including *Modern Man is Obsolete* (1945) and *Who Speaks for Man?* (1952). Since 1942 he has been editor of *The Saturday Review*.

OUT OF INNER NECESSITY

▶

by ALBERT EINSTEIN

HAVE hardly ever met a person in whom kindliness and
a yearning for beauty are so ideally fused as in Albert
Schweitzer. This is particularly impressive in someone who
is blessed with robust health. He enjoys using his arms and
hands in order to bring into existence what his nature urges
him to achieve. This robust health which demands immediate action has kept him from succumbing, through his moral
sensibility, to a pessimistic resignation. In this way he has
been able to preserve his joyfully affirmative nature, in spite
of all the disappointments which our time inflicts upon
every sensitive person.

He loves beauty, not only in the arts proper but also in the
sphere of the intellect, without being impressed by sophistry.
An unerring instinct helps him to preserve his closeness to
life and his spontaneity in everything. Everywhere he shuns
hardened and rigid traditions. He fights against it whenever
an individual by himself has any chance of succeeding. It
can be clearly felt in his classical work on Bach where he
exposes the dross and the mannerisms through which the
guild has obscured the creations of the beloved master and
impaired their direct and elementary impression.

It seems to me that the work in Lambaréné has been to
a considerable extent an escape from the morally petrified

and soulless tradition of our culture—an evil against which the individual is virtually powerless.

He has not preached and he has not warned and he did not dream of it that his example would become an ideal and a solace to innumerable others. He simply acts out of inner necessity.

There must be, after all, an indestructible good core in many people. Or else they would never have recognized his simple greatness.

A. Einstein

ALBERT EINSTEIN was born in Ulm, Germany, in 1879. He was educated at the Polytechnic School in Zurich, Switzerland He was professor at the University of Zurich, the German University in Prague, the Polytechnic School in Zurich, and the Prussian Academy of Science in Berlin He was awarded the Nobel Prize in 1922 He is the author of numerous technical papers and his more popular volumes include *Meaning of Relativity* (1923) and *Ideas and Opinions* (1954) Since 1933 he has been associated with the Institution for Advanced Study at Princeton, New Jersey.

PHILOSOPHICAL LEARNING AND MEDICAL SCIENCE

▶

by NOEL A. GILLESPIE

JANUARY 1955 marks the 80th birthday of Doctor Albert Schweitzer. All over the world men of goodwill will join in congratulating him and wishing well to him and his work. His name is become an household word. In honorary degrees and the Nobel Prize, the world has acclaimed his work for mankind. It is a safe statement that he is the most celebrated medical man in the world today because the conscience of the world has been stirred by his indomitable self-sacrifice and hard work. Having attained an international reputation as a philosopher, musician, and theologian at an early age, he acquired a medical degree and has since practiced medicine in a hospital of his own construction among the natives of one of the most backward races of men.

The original hospital at Andende, as I knew it in 1924, was not as imposing in appearance as an American institution for teaching and research. It was a small hut of galvanized iron with roof of thatch. Its equipment was primitive by modern standards. In one small compartment were the chemicals with which urinalyses could be conducted and in the main room was a microscope and the accessories necessary for the histological examination of blood. The new hospital of today is undoubtedly far better provided with the "tools of its trade," but—even so—it cannot compete with the luxurious and very expensive fittings of a large American institution. The equipment at Lambaréné is perfectly adequate to its task because the task itself is different. The hospital at Lambaréné exists to treat a sick person rather than a diseased organ or system of the body.

The layman of today is too prone to a blind worship of "Science" and medicine, particularly in America, is suffering from this tendency. To deal with facts which can be expressed with mathematical exactitude is easier and more rapid than to think carefully about abstract matters and reach a conclusion based on common sense. The right way to treat a bodily organ afflicted by a particular disease is easy to ascertain when once a correct diagnosis has been reached. Yet, in the wise words of Sir Robert Hutchison, we should "always remember that we are dealing with a sick man and not with an abstract disease." If we apply this principle, it will often be clear to us that the correct treatment of one particular organ may be useless and even unkind to the man himself. As Sir Robert says: "There is in the course of every mortal illness a stage beyond which further curative treatment is not only useless but even cruel."

It seems that the study of the humanities tends to stimulate an interest in one's fellow men, whereas those who pursue the exact sciences are chiefly interested in facts rather than people. In the last twenty years we have progressively eliminated from the requirements of a medical training the "intellectual" subjects, in order to gain more time for the consideration of scientific fact. The result is that young men today are less inclined to think of the patient as a person, and tend to regard him as a fascinating pathological condition to which a man is inconveniently attached.

Albert Schweitzer's attitude is the very antithesis of this. To him medicine is merely a tool: the means of expression of the philosophy and theology in which he has attained international fame. One simple remark of his made in Chicago in 1949 is much more penetrating than it seems at first: "The trouble with people nowadays is that they don't think enough." Philosophy and theology deal with the most abstract of ideas; Schweitzer's other outstanding activity has made him famous as an exponent of the greatest music yet written—that of J. S. Bach. For the first thirty years of his life, he pursued ultimate truth in abstract thought and ultimate beauty in sound. In a few years a mind of the calibre of his had little trouble in assimilating the facts necessary to become an efficient medical man. And for more than forty years he has put these gifts at the disposal of the natives of French Equatorial Africa.

The result of his work is such a stirring of men's consciences as to give him the unique position that is his on his eightieth birthday. If we apply his challenge to "think more," it will surely be obvious to us that Schweitzer is a great medical man more by reason of his philosophical learning than of his medical science. Let us apply his wisdom and realize that the individual patient is of more concern than the pathological condition of which he is the victim and that a medical student is a human being with qualities of character far more important than his "grade-point average." The best tribute that medicine can pay Albert Schweitzer on his eightieth birthday is to become more philosophical and reflective in outlook and practice.

Noel a. Gillespie

NOEL A. GILLESPIE was born in London in 1904. In 1924, as an Oxford undergraduate, he went to Lambaréné since, writes Dr. Schweitzer, "his mother entrusted him to me for a few months as a helper " He later received a doctorate in medicine from Oxford University and became a consulting anaesthetist in London, and Hon Asst Instructor in Anaesthetics at the London Hospital He later migrated to the University of Wisconsin, where he served as Associate Professor of Anaesthesia. He has had years of service with the Boy Scout Movement in both countries, and is active in Toc H and the Winant Volunteer Movement He has retired from medicine and lives in Madison, Wisconsin.

MEMORIES AND
MEDITATIONS:
1935-55

▶

by LADISLAS GOLDSCHMID

1935 ... From every part of the world, thousands of letters and numerous telegrams were sent to the little village of Günsbach, in Alsace. The press of all nations was publishing articles about a man already acknowledged for a long time as unique in his own field of artistry.

1935 ... The world was celebrating the 60th birthday of Dr. Albert Schweitzer. At this time I had already been working in the hospital established by him in the primeval forest of the Gabon.

Having recently returned to Europe on vacation, I again met *le Grand Docteur* in Lausanne.

We touched on many subjects and, having named persons that lived in the United States, I remember saying to him:

"Why don't you go, at least once, to the United States, so that you will know the 'New World' not only as a continent, but as a new world rich in personalities and in human qualities, thus enabling you to revise your impressions?"

As chance would have it, as I was saying these words, the Doctor held in his hand a telegram. It was an invitation that an American university had just extended to him.

Le Grand Docteur answered me: "I have now reached a

certain age. I have just passed sixty and I am beginning to age. I still have much to do. I no longer have time to make this trip. To become acquainted with new things would only add to my task, to say nothing of the obligations which would arise . . . Why increase the load that now weighs on my shoulders?"

He beseeched me to telegraph his negative answer. I carried out his instructions. Nevertheless, seeing him again later at his home, I could not help but say to him: "It would really surprise me if you did not go to America one day."

Twenty years have passed since that meeting at Lausanne. A great many of these years I have lived in Lambaréné, actually from 1933 to 1947.

Today, the world prepares to celebrate the 80th birthday of Dr. Schweitzer. In the meantime, *le Grand Docteur* has been to America and age has not slackened his drive or his stupendous vitality. That which he did not wish to do at sixty, he did at seventy-five.

The fourteen years that I spent at Lambaréné had a great influence on my life. Not only from the viewpoint of work, of living conditions, of broadening horizons, but over and above all, by the presence of *le Grand Docteur* himself.

It is principally during the years of the last war that his "presence" asserted itself for me.

Many of our aides departed. There were few of us left to assume the total burden of the work of the hospital.

I will always remember our conversations preceding the preparation for an operation while we disinfected our hands. So many tasks burdened us then that these instances took on an air of leisure. We chatted. I should say that I listened and felt the presence of a great man.

Here, I wish to say, that all during the time that the world was at war, and the hospital isolated, Dr. Schweitzer assisted

44

me in all my operations, preserving the untiring rhythm of his work, surmounting all difficulties, shortage of food, scarcity of medicine. This last problem was alleviated, thanks to the generosity of American friends.

Not for one day did the diversity of his usual schedule stop. He continued to write his manuscripts. He practiced on his piano specially made for the tropics.

I will never forget his unwavering optimism while he was always at work, in many different endeavors, accomplishing the tasks of several men. How many times did I hear him then affirm that evil cannot triumph in the world! He expressed symbolically that man is not yet ready to stop waiting for the Kingdom of God in his heart—that is to say, peace and harmony.

In 1947, I left Lambaréné to return to Europe with my wife and our little boy who was born there—this after an uninterrupted stay of nine years.

But the Doctor stayed at his post.

Some young doctors had come in 1946 to relieve him. He stayed with them to train them. Only when he was assured of the continuance of his work, when he was certain that no one would suffer by his absence, then only did he go back to Europe. He was seventy-two years old.

Why do I delve into the past? If I were asked, among all my countless recollections, which remains the most moving for me, I think I would assert: To watch the Doctor live.

Yes, then one understands that the secret of this extraordinary personality is sensitivity, consciousness of duty, developed to such a degree that it draws the moral and physical strength necessary to overcome all difficulties. And God knows he has had them! Added to all this is the blessing of making all his fellow workers profit by their association with him.

In analyzing his personality, I think we can say that it presents—because of its behavior, its awareness of duty, its convincing optimism, its courage, its goodness—such a radiance that it will certainly leave its mark on generations to come. I also think that the torch that he has lit should not go out.

The younger ones who come, and the pioneers who are still there, must live in this hope, must assert themselves in upholding this light. They must dissipate their own share of shadow from a sometimes ungrateful humanity which still is unable to understand and value a true greatness of soul.

The flame must not disappear, for the Doctor believes, and rightly so, in the capacity of humans to renew themselves in order to obtain the necessary ends, to propose new goals, new ideas. There can be an eternal transmutation, such as the Phoenix reborn from its ashes, thanks to the divine gift of love. Is not his philosophical doctrine of Reverence for Life, when put into practice, the most illuminating of examples?

While reflecting upon the Doctor, do not think of an inaccessible being, high on a pedestal, his head in the clouds. On the contrary, whatever it costs him in time and in labor, he is everyone's friend, a man caught up in everyday life, knowing how to scold, to storm sometimes, redeeming soon with a smile the necessary brusqueness of a preceding moment.

To rise to the heights one needs a variety of qualities independent of science, independent of experience, independent of work.

The Doctor has been laden with honors. We are used to enumerating the capacities and the titles of this extraordinary man, but the secret of his personality is hidden elsewhere.

All his creations, big as they may be, do not begin to tell the story.

His unique spirit which understands the suffering of the world and tries to console it and which proposes his un-shakable optimism, manifests itself in the reflection that he gives us. We must never forget the tasks and the duties with which civilization charges us.

The work and the sacrifice of Dr. Schweitzer—who never has been able to permit himself a personal life—must not be in vain. His message applies to all humanity and to serve it is to prepare the harvest for the future of time.

(This essay has been translated from the French by Miss Phyllis Fisher of Evanston, Illinois.)

LADISLAS GOLDSCHMID was born in Budapest, Hungary, in 1900. He was educated at universities in Strasbourg, Vienna, and Paris For several years he was a physician in French Equatorial Africa and now practices medicine in Nice, France. He was a member of the medical staff of Dr. Schweitzer's hospital at Lambaréné from 1933 to 1947.

THE PATTERN
OF PRESTIGE

▶

by GERALD HEARD

THERE is nothing more hopeful in the bewildered striving of our world today than the search for the hero, the pattern of prestige. It has been said that it takes three generations to incarnate an Avatar. The first generation is one of seekers: They express the need for a new contemporary manifestation of wholeness, of archetypal man and they define what such a one should be. In the second generation one is found of whom his finders say, "Come and see. This is he of whom the prophets spake." In the third he has passed from the temporal to the aeonic and century after century the individual will be abstracted from his character till only the type remains. Then once again the demand for immediacy will reassert itself against the tradition's claim to be self-sufficient. Seekers will ask: Finders will reply. And history's mysterious process of natural selection will extract, condense, define, reduce, and finally render obsolete. Something of this threefold process we may see, too, in the rise, recognition and stylization of the hero. And today the hero, though he neither makes nor has made for him the claims of the Avatar, is a more comprehensible idea, a more immediate stimulant to ordinary men. Incarnation (God coming down and taking human form) is now an idea as difficult for the psychologist and the scholar as for the engineer or executive.

48

While the hope that a man may rise to superhuman heights of performance and character, that hope today seems not only necessary but reasonable, heroic but possible and, if possible, rightly to be realized.

The ancient heroes need replacing not because they were not heroic. We have given up trying to debunk the real saints. Though they may be far fewer than the loaded calendars of orthodox communions would have us believe, there is throughout history a hard core of super heroes whose gold resists all the acids of satire, or the break-down analyses of the "nothing but" psychologies. We need new heroes now because we need new precedents. We need to know precisely what is heroic behavior in our unprecedented age. *What Would Jesus Do? If Christ Came to Chicago* were books easy to sell and easy to write up to the end of the last century. Now our knowledge of first century Judea as much as our acquaintance with mid-twentieth century mankind gives us pause. But we must have some guidance, some rulings today, some proofs by action that here is noble and imitable behavior in and for our age.

These people must be not merely supreme experts—an Einstein or a Niels Bohr—or amazing surmounters of limitation and handicap such as a Helen Keller. They must be reasonably like ourselves in generalized equipment and average freedom. They must be ordinary men of extraordinary dimension. Something like what we might have been had we had one other thing above what we have had—an unwavering sense of dedication. There have been three such in our time: Kagawa for Japan, Gandhi for India, and Albert Schweitzer for our Western tradition. And Schweitzer is the most communicable and so the one who as the days go on may prove to be the most significant. Significant (the word is used advisedly) because he can stand for a sign pointing where we

may find contemporary meaning. For he is the most generalized of these three heroic souls. Kagawa has mainly served
Japan, its interpreter, its inspirer—a bridge builder between
its intense social heredity and his deep devotion to our
Western Faith. Gandhi was in his home-spun "chuddar" a
symbol of his dream, a self-sustaining non-violent India.
Schweitzer is both more general and more intimate. A person
of presence, a "man of being," yet he has always been one of
ourselves, a big, strong, capable character head and shoulders
above us but standing on the same base as we. There never
was anything alien, still less self-consciously aloof, to startle
us. His greatness has been that of the masterpieces which as
quietly as the dawn convince us that all around is meaning
if we could only see. His gifts are greatly humane. First as
the scholar-missionary whose intense devotion to an almost
ruthless truth in no wise rendered less intense his dedication
to preach the Gospel to those to whom we had brought the
black news that they were our chattels. Secondly, as the
philosopher who has the station and poise to see history as
a whole and indicate "Reverence for Life" as the profoundest
guide for living. Thirdly, as the physician, he preaches by
practice the doctrine that body and mind are one, and shows
the charity which wins a hearing for truth by showing it can
defeat disease, and for the ideal by giving back the strength
without which the ideal cannot be pursued. Fourthly, as the
musician he manifests mastery in that art which has been
our troubled epoch's supreme contribution to the arts and
he interprets the master Bach who conveyed the message of
Protestant Evangelicalism with a supreme force which will
make it remembered when all its dogmas are in ruin.

Such then is the contemporary hero. Jesus gave offence by
eating with tax farmers and prostitutes. Schweitzer has been
blamed on numerous counts—from leaving Europe to go to

the Congo, when he should have stayed with his own agonizing continent, to dining with the company he chooses for his thorough conversation and letting his Africans dine happily with themselves. Certainly his post in Africa has not been isolation. The spiritual circuit riders of the globe all count Lambaréné as one of the important stages on the world course. And his very humanity preserves him from becoming either an aloof seer or a bland featureless host complying with everyone's instant demand that his behavior should in every respect be ruled by their notions of plastic amiability.

Here then we have heroism, the contemporary hero strong but not rigid, informed but not dogmatic, thoughtful, artistic and also constantly practical, with a philosophy that is gentle and a performance that is firm. Could we ask for a better pattern of prestige? Is not such a character not only a signpost pointing to the pass but a promise that it can be scaled?

Gerald Heard

GERALD HEARD was born in London in 1889. He was educated at Cambridge University. He was a commentator on science for the British Broadcasting Company from 1930-34 and came to the United States in 1937. Among his many volumes are *The Eternal Gospel* (1946) and *Is God in History?* (1949) He is a writer living in California. He met Dr. Schweitzer in London in 1936 and in Aspen, Colorado, in 1949.

DEAR
ALBERT SCHWEITZER

▶

by THEODOR HEUSS

ONORED guests! Dear Albert Schweitzer! Let me begin with a kind of personal discourse between you and me, in spite of the many listeners.

I should like to consider it not merely a pleasant coincidence, but a meaningful act of providence that we, on this occasion, stand face to face here today. It is now more than four decades since we first met one another. You were then the center of a very lively circle of friends in Strasbourg, a circle which I joined as a kind of peripheral figure.

Professionally, you were a remarkable phenomenon: you were a clergyman and lecturer in theology, you were about to take your first examination in medicine, and you had written a book about Bach which the experts in the field esteemed very highly. And every one of us was willing to abandon himself to the strong and sure power of your organ playing. Professionally, you were thus a "marvel" who could not but attract and interest the novice and yet it was amazing to the novice that in your circle all this seemed to be considered perfectly natural and normal. Your wealth of talent was simply a matter of course; one took it for granted. There was none of the solemnity about you which later sometimes seemed to threaten your life, but only *seemed*. The tension of your imminent departure from security into uncertainty was hardly noticeable. It was covered by the superior calmness and sense of direction that are part of your character.

You stood then before the great adventure of your life—to enter the hazards and wants of the jungle, to go to the poor Lazarus with the dark skin, with his diseases and epidemics and his agonies of soul. You would probably have rejected and brushed aside the word, "adventure," at that time, for the adventurer seeks power and gain and glory. You went into the service of infirmity, you chose a life of renunciation; and as fame began to fasten to you, after all, its lure failed to entice you. You knew a most unique way to de-personalize and objectify fame in your work—and the name of this work was Lambaréné!

Thus it was no adventure, but a great daring, not in quest of self-elevation but in the service of a cause. Within you, dear Schweitzer, there were planted and remained many potentialities, but I believe never those of the romantic, even though some would like to see you in a romantic light. In your memoirs, you mention that you had been "a dreamy child," but you became a man of very practical and concrete decision and of very wakeful awareness. A hazardous venture then: every genuine imitation of Christ is a hazardous venture. Did you intend thereby to set an "example"?

It may not have been unwelcome to you that the road by which your own heart was to find peace should in other hearts awaken unrest, though it brought not merely unrest but also consolation. For in the confounded and corrupted years, your name, your being, and your being the way you were, spelled calm and comfort for countless persons in the whole world.

. . . Don't expect me to attempt an all-inclusive appreciation. For that, my own qualifications are lacking. It would be a virtually mendacious presumption on my part if I

wanted to make pronouncements about the literary interpreter of Bach, or express comparative evaluations about the
musical theorist and practitioner of the organ. Nor am I a
theologian, for while I am an honorary doctor of theology,
this is not as obligating as it may seem. But I have the
distinct impression that if you, dear Schweitzer, had remained within the domain of philosophic theology as a
circumscribed field of your thinking, the theological development in Germany would probably—I say probably—have
taken a different direction. Ethics—which was and has remained the central issue of your thinking, not only your
acting—became dogmatically hardened into almost a kind of
"secularization of religion," as it is fashionably called. That
would not have been the case. Still, if I see correctly, even
out of your short activity in speculative theology, certain
matters have stayed alive and their traces in thoughtful
persons have not become lost.

Your book, *The Quest of the Historical Jesus,* in any case,
has out of a limited literary investigation developed into a
sublimated spiritual history of one hundred and fifty years
of Europe—this peculiar span from clean rationalism to
individual mysticism; clean rationalism—I calmly pronounce
the word, which for a few decades has been the damning
judgment for shortcomings.

I don't know how much effect upon you, dear Schweitzer,
when you were young, the example of Oberlin has had, the
Alsatian fellow-countryman of yours, whose poor Lazaruses
were not sitting in the Ogowe valley but in the valley of the
high and dry Vosges. Oberlin, to my feeling, is unthinkable
without the background of contemporary rationalism and,
at the same time, presents in his person—like others, too, like
Ph. M. Hahn—the not yet formulated interaction between
enlightenment and mysticism. Of him I was frequently re-

minded when I thought of you and the comparison has made me sense how much the vigorous nourishment of the eighteenth century is still effective in your makeup, if I interpret it correctly. This food stands at your table and is, it seems to me, richer in vitamins than dialectics and existentialism. These may be interesting as an intellectual training for the play of thoughts and imagination and for linguistic coquetries, but for the human relation between persons they are of no consequence. The Christian deed is more than the Christian view, and you are—because of your medical work in the jungle—forgiven for not having erected any theological dogmatics.

You have, however, standing between philosophy and theology, attempted to build a new foundation for ethics as the first prerequisite for human communion. You yourself have been, and are, not only an individuality but also an individualist, with a magnificent and also robust sense of freedom and the will for freedom. Your ethics is—to some this may sound strange—an individualist ethics. I believe the concepts of group, strata, class, race, even *das Volk* and *die Nation*—all these things or concepts have basically never interested you very much. Only individual men, individual fates, have done so. You did not go to the black people as a missionary seeking a mass effectiveness, but you have striven to help the Negro Joe—or whatever his name—in his helplessness . . . You have for such an attitude used the objectifying formula, "Reverence for Life." I should like to interpret it subjectively—out of *your* subjectivity—as the proud liberty to be humble before anything created; and this not in abstract irresponsibility, but in an ever-present, ever-demanding concreteness.

We have gathered here for the presentation of a peace prize. The word, peace, has many facets: peace of God, peace of evening, peace in labor relations—religious, sentimental, social meanings. But today—here, at this time—the word, peace, simply signifies the wish that not again shall there be war, that the grief which is man's companion shall be not a thousandfold, not a millionfold multiplied technologically. Is the word, peace, then, as used here, a political term? Is Schweitzer a politician? No—that he is not. He tells us, it is true, that as a youth he has read huge amounts of history, and history is the history of states, coagulated politics. But, if I interpret him correctly, he guarded himself against these things, as curious and eager for the knowledge of life as he was, so that he would not be distracted from his true life goal; but with all that, his own work, too, has of course often enough been touched by politics.

I shall now tell an anecdote. I hope, sir, you won't afterwards say it isn't true. Werner Picht has once told it. That Goebbels, with a remarkable lack of instinct, conceived the idea to bring this strange jungle doctor as still another attraction into his Germany to let him give organ concerts and lecture. Goebbels ended his letter with that cautious and tentative formula which you may remember, "with German salute!" You, Schweitzer, closed your letter of refusal with the majestic formula, "with Central-African salute!" That was not only irony but a superior—if, alas, ineffective—lesson.

I, myself, received about thirteen years ago a letter from you from Lambaréné which in very nice and friendly terms discussed my biography of Friedrich Naumann. For somehow you, too, felt an inner response to the phenomenon of that man who meant something for Frankfort, who made his entrance into German history from here. Now in that letter you made the remark that you had to detach yourself internally from Naumann in that discussion which had been carried on half a century ago and had concerned the Armenian people. Naumann had tried to justify political expediency, its primeval claim, against the pure ethics of love. I dug up this letter a few days ago. It contains the sentence about Naumann: "He forces himself to be different from what he by nature is." In this word, the eternal problem of a Christian kind of politics is sounded. Yet to treat of that is not the purpose of this hour, of these few minutes which are allowed to me. The remarkable thing is that Schweitzer is not a politician, but out of his metaphysical attitude grew a sort of spiritual politics. This, sir, was not your goal, but it is the result, a result of your life's work, and that in two spheres. For those of us for whom the German-French relationship has become the central European problem (or for those of us for whom it has always been thus) —and I mean not only a diplomatically and technically well-formulated relationship of legal paragraphs, but a matter of the psychological enlightenment of all souls—for those, Albert Schweitzer is a symbol today, the symbol of a man who took from both nations spiritually, who served both, enriched both, and who is loved in both. Beyond that—the road you took is unthinkable without your friends in Switzerland, without your friends in Scandinavia. And then the great march of conquest by love into the Anglo-Saxon world; in America, to be sure, the path was already partly paved by Quakerism which, in a certain sense, had pre-lived the ethical convictions of your attitude. The jungle hospital in French Equatorial Africa wants to belong to all, or all want to have a part in it. Well, Schweitzer could say: "But, my dear Heuss, I should have first sent my bookkeeper to you to give you a little information about how things stand regarding the world's wish to partake and assist." But you understand the point I want to make.

And now, once more, the eighteenth century. Then the

"citizen of the world" was invented. Later he was made into literature, in our time one has—I don't want to hurt anybody —organized and registered him. But here, in this man, the citizen of the world has lived, in concrete achievement without phrases . . .

(The above address was delivered on the occasion of the receipt, by Dr. Schweitzer, of a peace prize given by the Association of German Publishers and Booksellers in Frankfort on the Main on September 16, 1951. The original address used with permission from *Festschrift für Albert Schweitzer*, edited by Fritz Buri and published in 1955 by Paul Haupt, Berne, Switzerland. Translated from the German by Dr. Felix Pollak, Rare Book Librarian, Northwestern University, Evanston, Illinois.)

THEODOR HEUSS was born in Brackenheim, Germany, in 1884. He attended the universities of Munich and Berlin. At various times he was editor, author, and lecturer at Berlin's Political Academy He represented the old Democratic Party in the Berlin City Council and the *Reichstag* when the Nazis dismissed him from his public posts in 1933 After the war he became co-publisher of the Heidelberg newspaper, *Rhein-Neckar Zeitung* and later Minister of Education in Wuerttemberg-Baden He was chairman of the Free Democratic Party when, in 1949, he was elected President of the Federal Republic of Germany. He was re-elected to a second five-year term in July 1954. He is an old friend of Dr. Schweitzer.

"THE LION WHO
LAUGHS"—AND WEEPS

by ALLAN A. HUNTER

FTER his swim in an outdoor pool, a Californian noticed a half-drowned bee struggling. The man was cold and in a hurry and in a mood only for the hot shower. Then the imagined face of the great reverencer for life with his dedication, intervened: "Rescue an insect. Save it from being trampled on and you break down the barrier between yourself and life."

At the risk of being thanked with a sting the shivering man set his small neighbor free. Then he saw another and lifted it out of the water. But there were others. Finally he quit, murmuring to himself, "Maybe that's enough of Albert Schweitzer for one day." The impact of this man who is too outgoing for insecurity, or self-pity, or self-indulgence, cannot be measured. Thousands of us, to the degree that we have had contact with him, walk a little less rudely over this earth and its creatures.

My own contact, physically speaking, with this spiritual giant, is limited to an afternoon and evening with him at Aspen, Colorado. Generous friends, phoning from where he was a mile and a half high in the Rockies, had made the interview possible. One of them, late in his twenties, had said wistfully upon meeting him that same day, "I've often thought of being a doctor."

"Go ahead," smiled Schweitzer putting an encouraging arm around him. My friend is now, five years later, an M.D. himself.

It is part of Dr. Schweitzer's genius to make us little people believe in ourselves so that we really do "go ahead." They may say in Africa that he is paternalistic and that he doesn't train the black people to take sufficient responsibility as his colleagues. However that may be, here is one whom you can observe unmistakably making everybody within personal range feel at home because he himself is.

On the pipe organ he wins the applause of the world's ablest critics. He is an expert consultant, or used to be, on organ construction. He has put up a hospital in the jungle, doing some of the most complicated and hardest work with his own hands. He can cut out your appendix accurately. He is sympathy incarnate, yet his intellect is one of the toughest and most sophisticated among the philosophers of East or West.

You haven't met him yet, but in a few minutes he will be entering the cafeteria where you have taken up a strategic position to watch as you eat. Here he comes. Yes, Romain Rolland's phrase is apt: "the lion who laughs." At the same time the only man living in possession of a doctorate in music, another in theology, another in medicine, and still another in philosophy, makes you at first glance think of a half-drunk smiling sailor or maybe a tired bar-tender.

With tray in his hands he stops to chat a moment with the girl behind the cash register. He's under no pressure. He's living in the eternal now. While in that situation he acts as if she were the only person in the world so far as he is concerned. Will she, the rest of her life because of this brief electric experience of empathy, be more respectful toward wasps on the window pane trying to get out, and to fellow human creatures behind other cash registers?

Only twenty feet away, he is seated now between Mrs. Schweitzer and Dr. Emory Ross, the interpreter. Could those be lamb chops on the doctor's plate? They are, and he's enjoying them; but not for long. A student stands hesitantly, a pen in one hand, a book by the famous author in another. That is too much for the kindest of men. Up he jumps, pushes the student onto a chair beside a vacant table, sits beside him and proceeds painstakingly to autograph the book adding a personal message. In a moment a small crowd is around the table holding out their books to be signed. What wholehearted courtesy! But it's more than courtesy. The chops are cold before Dr. Ross is able to get him back to his own table.

Half an hour later in the back seat beside Mrs. Schweitzer, with the Doctor on the front seat and Dr. Ross at the wheel, I ask her for an accurate version of the rat story. With animation she tells how in their African cottage the rats were a problem. They didn't bother the doctor; he could sleep through anything. But she—they kept her awake at night. So she complained, once.

Very well, he would make a non-violent trap.

Early next morning she instructed a servant to put the captive rats and some heavy rocks in a sack, take the whole lot out on the Ogowe River, and drop them there to the bottom. The servant shortly returned. Mrs. Schweitzer was puzzled. How could he have done the job so quickly? "I was carrying the rats to the river," he explained sheepishly, "but the Doctor saw me. He said, 'Give them to me.' I did. Then he let them all out."

The rats came back,[3] of course. Later in the day Mrs.

Schweitzer stated the issue as clearly as she could. "My husband," she said, trying not to be exasperated, "I ask you: Which do you value more, those rats or my sleep?" The statuesque figure in the black coat on the front seat, continued to act as though lost in thought. If a martyr is one who lives with a saint, Dr. Schweitzer's wife certainly doesn't let the ordeal get her down.

He is so considerate of the life about him that in his presence you soon find yourself wanting to be considerate of *him*. That night, on the way back from dinner a few miles out of Aspen, I was sitting beside him. To make more room for him I squeezed up against the door of the station wagon. For several minutes there was silence. Then as if he knew how much I wanted to communicate without being a nuisance, he gave me a quick impulsive hug as if to say: "Thanks, brother, for not asking those fool questions I've been answering all day."

That night he invited me to his room to be with him while he made a recording, in French and then in German, of his famous lecture on Goethe. For nearly two hours he read his script into the microphone and cooperated with the radio people. While I waited, scene after scene out of a life much more exciting than Goethe's flashed across my memory . . .

When the radio men have gone, I also start to go. But Dr. Schweitzer is at the door before I am. He seizes my arm and forces me to sit beside him as he reclines on the couch. For several minutes he speaks in easy French. To think—and he grins spontaneously as a boy—that anyone should come all the way from California just to meet him! I make for the door. But he is there before me once again, warmly gripping me with that huge hand which with equal skill hammers nails into the hospital roof, sews up an incision, writes self-revealing letters and theological or philosophical books, or plays Bach to his gazelles on the old insect-proof piano.

He is tired, probably dead-tired, as he stands by the door; but his half-closed eyes are twinkling as he asks me whether I am sure, really sure, I know how to get back to my room. Fortunately, I do. Otherwise he would find out and nothing would stop him from escorting a fellow human being, none too certain of his way, through the dark.

The secret? Perhaps it is suggested through these words which Dr. Schweitzer was good enough to write with his own hand from Africa early in 1940: "When as a child I first heard of the Kingdom of God, I was profoundly moved. And always I have carried the thought of the Kingdom of God in my heart. I consider myself happy to be able to serve this Kingdom with thoughts and activities. Someday these thoughts will take root anew in the hearts of men. It is this certitude which gives me the courage to live in this day so terrifying to pass through."

Allan A. Hunter

ALLAN A. HUNTER was born in Toronto, Canada, in 1893 He was educated at Princeton University and Columbia University. He is the author of several volumes, including *The Audacity of Faith* (1949), and *Courage in Both Hands* (1951). Since 1926 he has been minister of the Mt. Hollywood Congregational Church in Los Angeles, California. In 1949 he met Dr. Schweitzer in Aspen, Colorado.

LIEBER BRUDER
ALBERT!

▶

by LOUIS MAYER

THIS is to bring you my greetings of love and fellowship, together with my congratulations upon your 80th
birthday. The entire civilized world will be acclaiming
and celebrating you as the man who, in spite of the troubled
waters on the sea of human relations, has sailed a true course
under the banners of all-embracing love and service to all.
I am the happier to join them because of the close attachment
with which I have been privileged. I know how you protest
the use of the words "proud" and "honor" in this connection
and yet I feel both proud and highly honored to be asked to
make a contribution to this Festschrift. You may never find
the time to read more than a morsel of it, just as you would
be able to eat only a small slice of the huge birthday cake,
to which the Festschrift may be likened.

"Brother at first sight" would not be quite right; for I well
remember how disturbed you looked when we first met, only
five years ago, after a funeral service in the Günsbach church.
On the strength of Charles R. Joy's assurance of a welcome,
I had gone to Europe especially to see you. But on my writing, immediately on arrival, there was no reply during the
thirty days my visa permitted me to stay in Germany at that
time. Two weeks later, in Switzerland, a postcard informed

me that you were still tired and unsettled, asking that I postpone my visit till the end of April. However, I decided to take a chance and at least see Günsbach. I arrived at the church while preparations for a Catholic funeral were in progress and was informed that you were in the village and expected to attend the service. When you entered, following the mourners, you chose the pew directly behind me. You did not seem too much pleased when I introduced myself. It was Mme. Martin who came rushing across the aisle. She had recognized me somehow. Beamingly she told me how fortunate I was to arrive just then and immediately she laid the plans for the next three days. It was not until I sat next to you at the organ during the Protestant church service on the following morning that the film of reserve dispersed—perhaps by my obvious familiarity with the first hymn, "Hallelujah, schöner Morgen," so befitting that glorious February Sunday morning, with the feeling of spring already in the air. I was "der liebe Amerikaner" when we sat at table together with Mme. Schweitzer for lunch on Tuesday noon, when the relief I was modeling while you were writing in your workroom was practically finished.

At Strasbourg, a week later, I was able to present you with the first plaster cast of the relief. The tête-à-tête visit, looked forward to, did not come about. Too many others were coming and going, but I was assured it would be better next time. I had my misgivings. In a Zurich bookshop, among other illuminated cards, I had picked up one with the first stanza of the foundation hymn by the Moravian leader, Count Zinsendorf: "Herz und Herz vereint zusammen." On my second visit to the Speichergasse, the reception room was so over-patronized, that I was ushered upstairs to Mathilde Kottmann's room, until the atmosphere might clear at tea time. When prospects improved, I was taken to the small room adjoining the reception room, where the carved wooden tablet bearing your quotation ("We must all help to carry the burden of woe which lies on the world") hangs over your bed. And there, all by myself, I was served tea! It had gotten to be six o'clock. There was only a minute left to see you when I was finally called, before you were to leave by car for some other prearranged appointment. I placed the Zinsendorf card, with something I had written on the back for this eventuality, into your pocket as a parting greeting, as we hurriedly shook hands in the still-crowded room. Next morning, before leaving Strasbourg, you called by telephone to verify the "Bruderschaft."

You have referred to this meeting of ours as being ordained by destiny. For me it led to the opening of many doors into a richer and fuller life ever since. How happy we were to meet again, when you and Helene arrived in New York, on your way to Aspen! I was delighted there, when you gave me the necessary instructions and asked me to substitute for Mme. Martin as corresponding secretary. And this I was glad to continue in your New York apartment until you returned to Europe.

Do you still remember the letter I wrote to the nineteen-year-old bundle of American impertinence? He was evidently of "good family" and had seen the number of *Life* that made you "the greatest man in the world." On very handsome stationery he sent his request for an autographed photograph as an addition to his collection of such illustrious personages as the Duke of Windsor and several Hollywood stars. There was neither a stamped return envelope nor a thought of your expenditure of time and money. He had evidently never read your story about the two potato sacks full of unanswered letters you carried back to Africa on one of your earlier trips. I wrote him a little sermonette on the difference between selfishness and service. I said the price of the photograph, plus postage, would probably pay for a bandage the Doctor could apply to a needy patient at his hospital at Lambaréné, which is sustained by voluntary gifts. Such gifts were received at the Albert Schweitzer Fellowship, 156 Fifth Ave., New York. When you came back to your room late that evening, after one of the receptions, I wanted you to OK the letter, before I sent it, and read it to you. "Just hold it," you said, "he will get the photograph also."

"You want to be like God Almighty and let your sun shine on good and bad alike?" I answered.

To which you quietly replied, "Yes."

You finally had to take the letter aboard ship with you to mail with others which you hadn't time to read and sign. I am sure your heaping of fiery coals on the boy's head by your kindness made a deeper impression than my sermonette. At any rate, your simple reply to me was a sermon I could not easily forget. Several years later you recalled the story remarking "and what a brushing you gave him."

Then I remember the striking experience of mental telepathy on the train from Glenwood Springs, after leaving Aspen. In exchange for the time I had devoted to you at Aspen, your time on the train was to be mine. Since we first entered the diner, you left me and the young doctor-organist in my company (who intended to follow in your footsteps and become a missionary doctor in the Far East) with the understanding that I was to look you up soon after lunch. I was telling the young doctor about a group of young people who had come to your room the day before, wanting to put some questions to you. But since you were in demand elsewhere at the time, they wanted me to tell them something about you. In many ways, I said, you resembled Eugene Debs, and quoted James Whitcomb Riley's lines:

"And here's 'Gene Debs, a man that stands
And holds right out in his two hands
As big a heart as ever beat
Twixt this earth and the Judgment Seat."

Didn't that sound as though it might have been written for Albert Schweitzer? You had been waiting for me, not in your comfortable Pullman compartment, but on the platform between two coaches, stooping over to look out of the window as we passed through the grand scenery of Colorado Canyon. I still had the Debs story in mind and wanted to tell you about it, when you received me with the question: "Did you know Debs?" Oh yes, that friendship between Debs and me was like that between Albert Schweitzer and me. It was a ray of light, not limited by time and space. Or, as Gene put it at our first meeting when he put his arms around me and kissed the top of my head, "Louis, I have known you for aeons and aeons."

Thereupon you surprised me with the statement that Eugene Debs was your mother's first cousin. I remembered that Gene's father had come to America from Colmar, Alsace. You told me how one of your American students at Strasbourg had described Debs to you in most depreciatory terms. I, in turn, pictured him more as a saint and champion of the underdog and mentioned that, after his death, I was asked to write a brief reminiscence in which I related three incidents which seemed to compare with similar ones in the life of Jesus. Then you became intensely interested and we left the platform to continue our conversation at length in your private compartment.

Perhaps it is not expedient to say too much about Debs in connection with you. Gene bore resentment to no one, not even to Pullman, who was the immediate cause of his first imprisonment, but Debs was vigorously denounced by those devotees of democracy who remain unaware of a class system within it. Appearance counts for so much in our world of affairs. I cannot help thinking of your traveling in Europe in a third-class railway coach "because there is no fourth," while here in America you were fated to travel Pullman in deference to your age and position. Still you were perhaps at one with Debs in his statement: "As long as there is a lower class, I am of it."

So many questions are asked about you: "When you meet a man like that, what do you talk about?" Some people think of you as completely wrapped up in a theory called "Reverence for Life" as is Einstein in his theory of "Relativity." It does not occur to them that Reverence for Life is only the concise tabulation for the guiding spirit of a disciplined life-long practice to do no evil and as much good as possible to every living creature. That dedication to service, to kindness, and good will, was already pronounced, when as a boy you saw the Colmar monument to Admiral Bruat, conqueror of French Equatorial Africa, with the cringing native on its base. You did not share the pride of the patriotic victor (as you were supposed to do), but sympathized with the vanquished and determined, at that early age, to devote your life to counteract this wrong and wicked "worldly" policy of survival of the fittest, practiced by Christians and barbarians alike.

What made you so "un-worldly minded," even then? And why was your first scholarly effort devoted to the "Quest of the Historical Jesus?"

I was deeply impressed by Werner Picht's choice of the quotation of yours, "Ich kreise um Jesus," as motto for his short, but profound, biographical sketch of Albert Schweitzer. What you say in that quotation ("I rotate around Jesus") seems to me as revealing as anything ever written about you. It is a dedication to pattern your life after that of Jesus, to spend it in selfless service, even if it involved sacrifice. It is because you remained true to that early decision that you stand out as a shining light among Christianity of today. You were not passively satisfied to accept the "Faith of our Fathers" as a taken-for-granted inheritance. But you heeded the advice of your great exemplar among the German bards, in his famous *Faust*: "Was du ererbt von deinen Vätern, erwirb es, um es zu besitzen." (What you inherit from your fathers, earn it, to possess it fully). After years of ardent study on this quest, you came into close associationship with a Jesus you had rediscovered and made your own—the Love of God personified, spreading it wherever you went. However, your early Christian training, your sensitiveness and simple, straight sincerity were important factors toward the great decision to follow the Spiritual Light around which you rotate. These marvelous hymns of the early Protestant era, glorified by the musical arrangement of Bach's genius, had already become part and parcel of you. "Jesu, geh voran auf der Lebensbahn" was not only to be sung at some Sunday service with the sanctimonious attitude of the Pharisee, but was to become the *Leitmotif* of your daily living. You were also aware of the demands of the world of today in which you were to serve. That called for the development of all the talents and faculties with which you were so richly endowed. One seemed to call forth and augment another. Also the activity in one seemed to furnish the necessary relaxation from another. Those of us who could be with you at close range could see how accumulated responsibility and fatigue vanished not only as soon as you were at the organ long enough to be lifted into the realm of universal harmony, but also after an hour's undisturbed, successful writing. This is the great secret of the unceasing energy needed for your self-imposed tasks.

And now the worldly world—which is as unChristian as ever, in spite of its many thriving Christian churches—acclaims you as its outstanding luminary and has awarded· you its most coveted distinction, the Nobel Prize. We Americans join the rest of the world in looking to the Great Doctor for a prescription to cure the nervous excitement caused by international strife and constant threat of war. You have not only rewritten the prescription Jesus gave in his day ("Love ye one another, even your enemies"), you have asked them to use their minds and be convinced that this actual practice of goodwill is the only hope for our cure and our survival. "Reverence for Life" may remain a theory for the world at large, which is run by "Politics," with which you claim "to have nothing to do" but which you do influence after all. When all the blustering challenges and counter-challenges have become stale, sanity will prevail and you will have contributed a large share in its victory to establish Peace on Earth.

"Jesu, geh voran auf der Lebensbahn
Und wir wollen nicht verweilen
Dir getreulich nachzueilen;
Führ uns an der Hand, bis ins Vaterland."

Brother Louis

LOUIS MAYER was born in Milwaukee, Wisconsin, in 1869. He studied art at Weimar, Munich, and Paris. He was a contributor of art columns to several Milwaukee newspapers and is known as the Dean of Wisconsin painters and sculptors. Since 1913 he has lived in New York State and has maintained a studio for painting and sculpturing. In 1949 he met Dr. Schweitzer and has had contact with him ever since.

ALBERT SCHWEITZER:
REFORM, REVOLUTION
REGENERATION!

▶

by G. BROMLEY OXNAM

STRICTLY speaking, Albert Schweitzer is not a social reformer. Unlike Sidney and Beatrice Webb—whose researches and teaching, personal leadership, and influence were chiefly responsible for the setting up of powerful educational institutions, propaganda bodies and a political party, and whose lives contributed to the reform that marked the passing of Britain from a capitalist to a socialist society—Schweitzer has spent most of his years in a faraway mission station. True, his scholarship has been recognized, but he has not released a movement such as Walter Rauschenbusch did in his proclamation of the social gospel, nor has he administered such vast reforming enterprise as David Lilienthal did in the Tennessee Valley, or been charged with responsibility such as that resting upon the chairman of the Atomic Energy Commission. No nation has waited breathlessly upon his word. No people has bowed to his will as did India when, upon a bed in a prison cell, Gandhi fasted both as penance and persuasion, risking all upon the power of love to transform.

No people has been freed because of Schweitzer's labors. None the less, he stands as a social reformer, changing the thinking of men by the sheer power of his example, a servant in the house, whose influence cleanses of iniquity. Men whom he has never met are asking, Is this the Way? Are talents a trust? Is life found by losing it? It is the reforming power of a great example. He judges no man, but his life forces every man to judge himself. He does not shout, "Abolish the exploitation of man by man." He goes to Africa to give himself as a part payment on a debt to the black man, who has been exploited. He does not talk of "classless society." He serves the least of these. And he stands strong in the storm of sacrificial service. The winds of adversity have beat upon him, and the bright light of God's approval has shone upon him. He has borne physical burdens and suffered anguish of the spirit. But he has carried on with light in his eyes, laughter upon his lips, strength in his soul; and men have seen and wondered. His influence moves quietly across the seas. Strong men ponder, lives are changed, and the changed move into society for further change. A man in the forest, a surgeon with a knife, a musician at the keyboard, a scholar with his books, but more, so much more, a man of God who affirms love and life, and reforms.

Strictly speaking, to repeat, Schweitzer is not a social reformer. True, a section of Africa was changed, but no party marches under his leadership, no bill in Congress bears his name, we do not hear of the economics of Schweitzer nor of the political principles of this missionary. But he does reform. He closes his autobiography with an observation: "If men can be found who revolt against the spirit of thoughtlessness, and who are personalities sound enough and profound enough to let the ideals of ethical progress radiate from them as a force, there will start an activity of the spirit which will be strong enough to evoke a new mental and spiritual disposition in mankind." He stands among his fellow-workers and beside them he serves, a personality sound enough and profound enough, and there radiates from him a force that has already started an action in the realm of the spirit that in the name of his Lord means change, the change that is reform, the reform that is regeneration.

Yes, he is profound enough. He writes: "Christianity cannot take the place of thinking, but it must be founded on it." Yes, he is sound enough. He says: "The essential element in Christianity as it was preached by Jesus and as it is comprehended by thought, is this, that it is only through love that we can attain to communion with God. All living knowledge of God rests upon this foundation: that we experience Him in our lives as Will-to-Love."

Reverence for Life, Reverence for Life, Reverence for Life —this is the theme of the great symphony that is Schweitzer. He knows that the modern state can only be cleansed if a new spirit rules. "Let us, then, undertake to drive the modern state, so far as the power of our thought reaches, into the spirituality and the morality of the civilized state, as it should be in accordance with the conception of Reverence for Life. . . . With confidence in the strength of the civilized spirit and temper which springs from Reverence for Life we take upon ourselves the task of making this civilized state an actuality . . . a state guided by an ethical consciousness."

A missionary marches on. And out of his life and thought, from the edge of the primeval forest and the forest hospital at Lambaréné, there has come a philosophy for civilization; and the quest for the historical Jesus has ended in the greatness that becoming a servant brings. There must be preparation in the heavens, the practice of great choirs, awaiting the coming some day of a man of music, and of science, and of thought, who will sit at the organ to accompany the heavenly host as it sings, "Glory to God in the highest, and on earth peace and good will among men."

His is the reform and the revolution wrought by regeneration!

G BROMLEY OXNAM was born in Sonora, California, in 1891 He was educated at the University of Southern California and Boston University He was ordained in the Methodist Episcopal ministry and was a faculty member at the University of Southern California and Boston University. He was president of De Pauw University from 1928-36 and Methodist Bishop of Omaha, Boston, and New York. He was one of the presidents of the World Council of Churches Among his many volumes are *Preaching in a Revolutionary Age* (1944), *Personalities in Social Reform* (1950), and *I Protest* (1954) Since 1952 he has been Methodist Bishop of Washington, D C

FOR WHOM RELIGION
IS A REALITY

▶

by SARVEPALLI RADHAKRISHNAN

I AM glad to have this opportunity of paying my tribute of admiration to the many-sided activities of Dr. Albert Schweitzer. I have been a student of his writings for many years and can testify to their great importance and wide influence.

What appeals to me specially is his insistence on spiritual religion. The great prophets of the world call upon us to seek the truth and practice of love. I remember a sentence in Schweitzer's early writings, where he says that rationalism free from assumptions ends in mysticism (I am quoting from memory). Mysticism requires us to bring about an inward change. The human being must be made into a new man. He is the raw material for an inner evolution. As he is, man is incomplete, imperfect, unfinished. He has to reach inner completion through a new understanding. This completion, this renewal, cannot be achieved by outer compulsion. Man must evolve by his own insight, in and from himself. This is the meaning of repentance, *meta-noia*.

There is no such thing as an automatic evolution of man. His development does not happen according to the laws of heredity and natural selection. It is bound up with conscious effort. Those who have evolved or realized their latent possibilities serve as examples and guides to others.

The practical outcome of inward evolution, of insight into

reality, is reverence for all life. Brotherhood of life becomes our ethical norm. *Abhaya* and *ahimsā,* in the words of the Upanishads, *prajñā* and *karuna* in the words of the Buddha, understanding and compassion, wisdom and love are the central simplicities of religion. Love God and love your neighbor, says Jesus.

Many of us who profess to be religious are only nominally so. Religion is, with most people, a matter of inheritance and good form. We aim at conformity, play for safety and pay our allegiance to the State or the surrounding mores. Religion is not a burning conviction which transforms our whole life and frees us from narrow group loyalties. When we come across a great spirit for whom religion is a reality, not a profession, we salute him. Such a one who deserves our homage is Albert Schweitzer. May his life and example inspire us to lead truly religious lives.

S. Radhakrishnan

SIR SARVEPALLI RADHAKRISHNAN was born in 1888. He was educated in Madras He became Vice-Chancellor of Benares Hindu University and, from 1936 to 1952, Spalding Professor of Eastern Religions and Ethics at Oxford University. He was Indian Ambassador to the U.S.S.R. from 1949 to 1952 He is the author of a number of volumes, including *The Hindu View of Life* (1927), *An Idealist View of Life* (1932), *Eastern Religions and Western Thought* (1939), and was editor of the collection, *Mahatma Gandhi* (1939) Since 1952 he has been Vice-President of the Republic of India.

ALBERT SCHWEITZER

▶

by MAGNUS RATTER

ALBERT Schweitzer is an ordinary man doing extraordinary things. Inspiration is not lacking but it is sweat and purpose, hallowed by consecration, that make him great.

Followers of great men are often bores because, other than in piety, we dislike untempered adulation: we prefer to meet our great men in their garden togs rather than in formal dress. If sin makes hotter news than goodness the biographer of Schweitzer is at instant disadvantage. There are no red passages: little Freudian, little Marxian, nothing to hate. His life story is as simple and natural, as pastoral and elemental as a field of buttercups. His life story never startles, if related as it unfolded. His biography, like the Mississippi in broad sure majesty, just goes rollin' on: fed by his numerous tributary interests.

His own *Life and Thought* is still better than any biography, for to write adequately of him is a big job. To set his many activities into the decades that give them birth, to show how much he was part of yet in advance of his time, to relate this to his sixty years of public service, then to set all within the mental spiritual development of Albert Schweitzer, who will or can do this?

Maybe the writer is now doing his schoolboy essay. Not always yet often the task creates the man.

*　　*　　*

It was the task that created Schweitzer. Heredity and environment provided the apt worker. He was born in The Manse, a handicap or a very good start. He enjoyed his boyhood where French and German cultures shook hands: better still, he said his prayers where Luther and The Pope lived in one church: best of all he came when modern man was about to find his soul.

Moulded, as much as he moulded, he became the spiritual voice of United Europe: the spiritual precedes the political.

To write an adequate life story the writer must be versed in European literature, music, theology, philosophy, tropical medicine, agriculture. He must not overwrite lest he be false: he must not underwrite else he will be dull. He must make simple words speak difficult thought in thrilling manner. This needs art.

*　　*　　*

The biographer must know his Goethe, Wilhelm Meister as well as Faust, with knowledge of Chinese and Indian thought, else he will not be able to appraise why Schweitzer remains a Christian, as assuredly he does. To write this so that the reader does not need a cup of tea needs skill.

To take him too far from the common life of Alsace would be wrong. He is the peasant thinking hard. He knows much that the clever have written, can create erudite phrases of his own, yet the mud of God's Acre is thick upon his boots. He remains a peasant thinking on death—and life: he is western history giving birth to a new idea.

As a father and grandfather, he is normal. His daughter

on her way to the dentist says, "Look, there's Daddy." This must be told, with affection but little sentiment.

As a husband, sharing intellectual companionship, listening to a bright young lady comment on his writings, as a doctor sharing a life of hardship with the trained nurse, this must all be related, but with reticence: he never wears his heart upon his sleeve. But Madame Schweitzer must be in the picture else it is not an adequate portrait.

To subordinate all this to his spiritual development is a difficult yet essential work if he is to survive his death. No one lives in history unless others keep alive his life and thought. Saints are sanctified in the memory of man by the writers who tell the story in the vernacular of later days.

*   *   *

It is desirable that someone show how he led the Christian Church to a full awareness of the Jesus of History: Jesus as he might have been interviewed by Reuter. But he has done more. He showed Paul leading the Jesus of Galilee into history. This is his abiding theological work. We see The Early Church think its way through the thought of the time till it fashions a redemption that will elevate the centuries.

No writer has come within ten miles of doing this.

*   *   *

Whether Schweitzer is too fast or too slow in playing Bach will never be settled. Tempo is taste. From Russian funeral music to American jazz is only an aeroplane trip these days.

As an authority on organ-building, he may create a new ear in Europe which may ask for new instruments. Or a new awareness of the truth in his emphasis may send thousands to listen to Bach on the old organs. In either instance his work will have served well.

As an interpreter of Bach it will be long before he is superceded. Any writer who would show the whole Schweitzer must give chapter and verse concerning Bach appreciation in 1910, then show how change came as a result of his book. That he gave Bach as a pictorial musician to Europe is known but it is not so well known how he changed the musical appreciation of his generation.

* * *

It may be that the young doctor in Lambaréné did not fully realize what his philosophy tries to do. It may be that this awareness, as it has deepened, is reason why the third volume delays its coming. Like the aging Goethe, his grasp of the universal is now so vast that he can scarce complete, to his satisfaction, his second part.

As a history of western thought, every chapter of his *Ethics* is a Baedeker guide to the thinkers of a century, yet always with direct intent. He does not lead through a dead museum: he shows the living past, raises thinkers from their graves, gently sets them back again, then sets forth his own view of life and mystery.

Chapters eighteen to twenty-two are Albert Pilgrim setting out toward a wicker gate. Only tomorrow can give judgment if this book, with its third volume still hung on the line, will go via the market stall to the pulping mill, or will become the moral content of numerous schoolbooks read by the grandchildren of modern man.

* * *

This present writer finds but one fault in him: it is serious. He tells that people today are a poor lot. Yet this wrongness is but tribute to his earnestness.

It is doubtful if modern war kills as high a percent of people as were killed by war in earlier centuries. On other counts this generation is worthy, kind, even generous. The victors were fair to the defeated. Modern man is kind to animals, poverty is almost whacked, pain is being overcome. All this is good.

Our generation may not take the good conduct prize from history yet we are not the dunce, or blackguard, of the fifty generations we know. Best evidence of widespread goodness is the strong admiration of Schweitzer, and the many others like him.

*　　*　　*

Some years ago this present writer went to Strasbourg to collect stories. He found but one story, for Schweitzer is as normal as most folks in the telephone directory. A simple home opened wide its door when it knew the visitor's intent. The woman could tell nothing about their young parson, by that time age fifty and famous, other than that, in the intimacy of their home, he prayed like The Savior.

This unknown writer must show him as a good parson, like many parsons, doing a humble job well, chosen, much to his surprise, for world fame. But the young man that bore the mark of God upon his brow was simply a hard-working parson who preached short sermons.

*　　*　　*

If Madame and Dr. Schweitzer should read this essay they would smile: then the old Doctor would wink, he is master of the wink. Yet if this present writer could go again to Günsbach unannounced, with remarkable facility for names and faces, the old man would smile welcome and Madame would be gracious.

Together, the old Doctor and the visitor would walk by night, in silence, aware of Kant's twin values. Quietly they would go to The Church: there, Bach would be played.

Rising early in the morning, ever a peasant, remembering

the last work of Faust, Schweitzer would pack his bag that he might return to Lambaréné, there to turn the wilderness into an orange grove, taking pain from the suffering native, with especial care for the leper, the insane, and the animal world.

No one who understands Schweitzer asks why he went to Africa. Good as his four books are, Lambaréné is greater. Wisely, history is as interested in act as in ink.

* * *

In a time when not all writers set the halo upon the forehead, when biography is often brilliant as Hollywood but is not all sunlight, it is health-giving to know that one writer was doing a sound job of hard work in a hot place. Few friends, in 1918, thought he would see 1955, much less be a world name.

In a time when some writers indulged a self undress, he wrote with an objective discipline concerning his private life that is Hebraic in its austerity: and very satisfying. Finally, readers are drawn to goodness though fascinated by sin.

* * *

If this unknown writer could exfoliate the three seeds Schweitzer has germinated he would do a service.

A new awareness of Jesus comes slowly to life, its central themes, The Good Samaritan and the Prodigal Son, neighborly and family love: political implications in the one, mystical meanings in the other. The Lord's Prayer and The Beatitudes must return to their own century before they come back to this century with fresh aptness.

Piety now finds new meanings in the last words of Jesus, "My God, why hast Thou forsaken me?" An experience that repeats itself, in differing historical setting, in every generation: from Jerusalem and Calvary to Gettysburg and The Theatre is a direct journey.

Through music modern man now enters into a world where nationalism, color prejudice, and personal sin do not exist. More than ever a few people enjoy aural dreams while many concert goers follow the architectonic in music; whereas the multitude can, as yet, only enjoy the melody.

In his work on Bach, Schweitzer has done more than write the story of a musical life, he has done more than show that architecture is frozen music, music is flowing architecture. He has made clear a new dimension in aesthetic experience.

*   *   *

Near to sending atomic power on peaceful mission, at the very moment of making obsolete coal and oil, modern man finds his life purpose rephrased: inner perfection is shown to lead to social responsibility.

If man is an animal that thinks about yesterday, today, tomorrow—history, mysticism, prophecy—he can no longer think that a good God created the bees because they give honey, a bad God created the mosquitoes because they carry malaria. Modern man must think out a modern faith, setting good and evil in their true relationship in the human, animal and mineral kingdom always aware the kingdoms blend at the frontiers.

In the philosophy of Reverence for Life, with an apt but not a final phrase, Schweitzer has given us an overall look at God and Man. If validated in the spiritual life of the future, it will come so because the teaching was supported by a life. Philosophers are many: good lives are many: on occasion, in history, when these two are one, a city, a people, a culture, moves up one class in the Sunday School of Life.

Schweitzer neither desires to be, nor ever can be made, the

founder of a new sect. There is no vast exaggeration upon which sects are founded. His thought is common sense, consecrated: his life is but average, dedicated. He is never Calvin: the decades will say if he is greater than or like Castellio: only the centuries can make other verdicts.

An adequate biography must make clear that the soul of his moral being was the three-fold sacrifice, that the spirit of his entire life was the early consecration at age twenty-one. His mental gifts, his artistic skill, these were but servants to his moral will. If he is to be given spiritual accolade, someone must tell, in final simplicity, how a man and his wife, made sacrifice—ever conscious that it was not a greater sacrifice than that made by countless others.

Only schoolboys want a hero; now that modern man lays aside his mediaeval schoolcap he asks only for representative men. Schweitzer is our member in the Spiritual Parliament of Mankind. Many today have voted him there.

MAGNUS RATTER was born in 1899 He was educated in Edinburgh and at Manchester College, Oxford He has been minister of Unitarian churches in London and Lancashire and has travelled in Germany and India as an emissary of liberal religion He is the author of *Albert Schweitzer* (1935), which was republished in a new, enlarged edition in 1950, and of *O Clouds Unfold* Since 1951 he has been minister of the Free Unitarian Church of Cape Town, Union of South Africa. He has been interested in Dr. Schweitzer for thirty years and met him in London, Gunsbach, and Edinburgh.

REVERENCE FOR LIFE:
AN INTERPRETATION

▶

by GEORGE SEAVER

WHAT is the most elementary experience of which consciousness is capable? It is the experience of existence: "I am alive." But sentience is impossible without awareness, which is cognition in germ; and both are impossible without desire, which is volition in germ. Self-realization, self-preservation, self-expression—these are together one. Thought, feeling, will—they are inseparable aspects of the same primary conscious experience. When thought deepens it becomes reflection; when feeling intensifies it becomes emotion; when the will strengthens it becomes conation.

But self-consciousness is impossible without consciousness of another or of others to which it stands over against. Hence with the subjective experience of self-existence comes the simultaneous objective corollary: "I am life that wills-to-live in the midst of other life that wills-to-live." From this there follows a grimly appalling consequence. For the world is so constituted that life, in order to maintain itself, must do so at the expense of life other than its own. "The world is a ghastly drama of will-to-live divided against itself. One existence makes its way at the cost of another; one destroys the other." In the evolutionary struggle for existence it is only the fittest that can survive; the weaker perish or are ruthlessly destroyed or actively preyed upon. This is true of life at every phase, not only in every realm of the animal and vegetable worlds but also in that of the human. For the course of human history, present as well as past, is very much a reproduction of the course of natural history: in both the Other is obtruded as something alien to the Self.

But man is not merely a more highly intelligent, sensitive, purposive kind of creature than the rest of creation. When he has grown to full self-consciousness he finds himself possessed of tendencies and ideals which differ from theirs, which in fact run counter to theirs. In him and in him alone thought becomes rational, feelings become compassionate, and his will moral. In other words, it is in the nature of a human being when he is truly human to be humane, that is, ethical: to develop all his faculties to their topmost bent in a spirit of self-reverence, and at the same time to regard with reverence and to assist all other existences which come within the range of his influence to develop theirs.

"The essential nature of the will-to-live is determination to live itself to the full. It carries within it the impulse to realize itself in the highest possible perfection. In the flowering tree, in the strange forms of the medusa, in the blade of grass, in the crystal; everywhere it strives to reach the perfection with which it is endowed. In everything that exists there is at work an imaginative force, which is determined by ideals. On us, beings who can move about freely and are capable of pre-considered purposive working, the impulse to perfection is given in such a way that we aim at raising to their highest material and spiritual value both ourselves and every existing thing which is open to our influence."

In the sub-human creation the primary instinct of self-preservation carries within it an inherent impulse for self-assertion in order to realize its potentialities and attain to ultimate self-perfection, and thus brings about a condition of unconscious or semi-conscious conflict with other existences which are striving towards the same end. In man, and in man alone, self-realization is paradoxically attainable only through a measure of self-sacrifice. He feels the life of the creaturely world outside him to be an extension of his own life. This involves him in a world—and life-affirmation which militates against his individual will-to-live, and therefore in an ever-increasing degree in a discipline of self-denial. In him the experience of outward conflict is replaced by one of inner tension. The primary instinct of self-preservation, on the natural sub-human level, is on the rational human level transformed into a will to enhance and promote the life of all that lives—even, if need be, at the expense of his own. Yet paradoxically, his individual will-to-live is not thereby diminished; rather it is enhanced.

"He will feel that all life's experiences are his own, he will give it all the help that he possibly can, and will feel all the promotion of life that he has been able to effect as the deepest happiness that can ever fall to his lot. . . .

"Existence will thereby become harder for him in every respect than it would be if he lived only for himself, but at the same time it will become richer, more beautiful, and happier. It will become, instead of mere existence, a real experience of life."

Reverence for Life is thus the interpenetration of the ethic of self-perfection with the ethic of self-devotion to others. The standard of the latter is external and objective; looking to the goal of action, it asks: what is the ultimate *Good?* It is essentially active and life-affirming. The standard of the former is internal and subjective; looking to the motive of the agent, it asks: what is the absolute *Right?* It is essentially passive and life-denying. But life as it is lived is a mixture of action and passion; and the nearer a human being approximates to sanity, the more equal in him is the blend of extravert and introvert. Reverence for Life is the bridge, not only between two mutually exclusive schools of moral philosophy, but also between two antagonistic psychological types.

The supreme consummation which the ethic of self-perfection sets before itself is this: to attain union with Infinite Being. This is Mysticism. It is the consciousness, whilst still amid the trammels of the finite and the temporal, of belonging to the infinite and the eternal. But it is only in the former that the latter is revealed. Infinite Being is not an abstraction, not a theoretical Essence.

"There is no Essence of Being, but only Infinite Being in infinite manifestations. It is only through the manifestations of Being, and only through those with which I enter into relation, that my being has any intercourse with Infinite Being. The devotion of my being to Infinite Being means devotion of my being to all the manifestations of being which need my devotion, and to which I am able to devote myself. . . .

"I am thrown indeed by Reverence for Life into an unrest such as the world does not know, but I obtain from it a blessedness which the world cannot give. . . . . I find myself in an inexpressible and surprising happiness of freedom from the world, and I experience therein a clearing of my life-view."

It is true that there is such an experience as the mysticism of identity with the World-Soul; but this is really no more than a mysticism *in vacuo*; it is purely subjective, lacking an ethical content. There is also a spurious kind of ethic which has, not a directly personal, but a sociological reference; but genuine ethics cannot be regarded as "the centre of a city whose main thoroughfares lead to the residential suburbs of social well-being." Reverence for Life is ethical mysticism. It is ethical because it recognizes its kinship with all that lives, and gives to all other existences the same respect that it gives to its own. It is mystical because in union with Infinite Being alone it finds its own completion, a union which however can only be realized in active participation with the life-destinies of other finite existences in the realm of phenomena. In biblical language ethical mysticism is expressed in two great commandments: to love God with one's whole soul, and to love one's neighbor as oneself. These two fundamental duties stand or fall together; the one implies the other; the one is impossible without the other. In obeying them man fulfills the purpose for which he was created; and in doing so he enters into the peace which passes understanding.

"All deep philosophy, and all deep religion, are ultimately a struggle for ethical mysticism, and mystical ethics. . . . Ethics are responsibility without limit towards all that lives. . . . Only an infinitely small part of Infinite Being comes within my reach. The rest of it drives on past me, like distant ships to which I make signals they do not understand. But by devoting myself to that which comes within my reach and needs me, I make spiritual inward devotion to Infinite Being a reality, and thereby give my own poor existence meaning and richness. The river has found its sea. . . ."

What is the determining factor of this ethic, that which gives it its power and its inspiration? It is pity. "Ethics are pity. All life is suffering . . ." Man can never be truly ethical as long as he regards himself and his fellows as, so to speak, the only pebbles on the beach of the eternal shore; as long as he maintains an attitude of aloof detachment from anything that lives, as long as he adopts the passive role of spectator, and not that of active participant, in the universal tragedy of life. For this would be to do himself an injury; to stifle himself, to deprive himself of the very breath of his being. But once he accepts his kinship with, and responsibility for, all creatures great and small; once he realizes that they, too, are the concern of the same Creator and the objects of His care, he experiences within him an unburdening, a release, and a sense that he has a right to his own place in the same universe. Reverence for Life engenders a new-found sensitivity which to conventional morality may well appear extravagant. All life is sacred to him. By going out of his way to rescue life, however apparently insignificant, he is paying a debt of honor to the Author of life, including his own.

Nevertheless, the world is so constituted that ethical man is laid under the cruel law of necessity whereby he must sacrifice other life in order to preserve his own. And not only so, but also to destroy life in order to preserve other life which he deems to be of higher value. The act of destruction can never be felt by a human being as an ethical act; it can only be felt as a necessity "within the realm of expedience." To preserve, maintain, and enhance life is to act "within the sphere of the ethical." It is a free, constructive, beneficent activity. This conflict between the ethical and the expedient, between freedom and necessity, between spirit and nature, constitutes a perpetual tension in our lives as inhabitants of a universe in which natural law does not correspond with spiritual law, and the world of fact is often incompatible with the world of values. It is for us to recognize the existence of this incompatibility, and to strive so far as in us lies to reduce this tension by realizing our debt to other lives which we sacrifice to our own.

In the assessment of the degree to which man is justified in taking life or inflicting pain to preserve his own life or another's, Reverence for Life lays down no scale of values: "It does not keep in store adjustments between ethics and necessity all ready for making up."

"In ethical conflicts man can only arrive at subjective decisions. No one can lay down for him at what point, on each occasion, lies the extreme limit of possibility for his persistence in the preservation and promotion of life. He alone has to decide, by letting himself be guided by a feeling of the highest possible responsibility towards other life . . .

"Those who experiment with operations or the use of drugs upon animals, or inoculate them with diseases, so as to be able to bring help to mankind with the results gained, must never quiet any misgivings they feel with the general reflection that their gruesome proceedings aim at a valuable result. They must first have considered in each individual case whether there is a real necessity to force on any animal this sacrifice for the sake of mankind, and they must take the most careful pains to ensure that the pain inflicted is made as small as possible."

This, be it remembered, is the considered verdict of a man who, as a surgeon and a scientist, is in his own words "a mass-murderer of bacteria;" who, as a medical missionary in the pest-infected swamps of West Africa, carries on an unceasing war with termites, mosquitoes, spiders, scorpions, snakes, leopards, and all the noxious vermin that endanger human life—and none more vigorously, determinedly, and deliberately than he; and yet who goes out of his way to lift a parched earthworm from the dust and put it safely in the grass, or stoops to rescue a struggling insect from a puddle, who tears no leaf from a tree and plucks no flower, and who prefers to work in the stuffy atmosphere of a shuttered room rather than let a moth flutter to its death round a lamp. As has been well said by another: "Reverence is a mental attitude; it is the opposite of ruthlessness, and of thoughtlessness. One can weed a garden reverently, or ruthlessly. This principle does not say it is a sin to pluck a flower or kill a moth; it says, do not pluck flowers or kill moths without first greeting the divine principle in them. No practical guidance? Anyone may be surprised how much such an acceptance of responsibility may enrich his spirit in an hour."

Great as are the responsibilities of the ethical man to the rest of creation, they are small in comparison with those which Reverence for Life imposes upon him in respect to his fellow men. Here his responsibility is "so unlimited as to be terrifying." Here also, the extent of his self-maintenance, justifiable in the midst of other life that wills-to-live, is not something to be determined *a priori* by any rule, but only by the absolute ethic of self-devotion applied to each situation as it arises: "How much of my life, my possessions, my rights, my happiness, my time, and my rest, I must devote to others, and how much of them I may keep for myself." On the economic level, Reverence for Life requires of the ethical man that he should regard nothing as exclusively his own. He knows that he is a steward of God's gifts, not a possessor; a trustee, not an owner. But in the administration of his trust, he is absolutely free; he is subject to no law imposed from without. The same is true in the matter of social "rights." The ethical man is unaware that he possesses any rights; he recognizes that he is a debtor, and knows only duties. He sees all life as one, his own life incorporate in the life of others, the lives of others incorporate in his own. In this there is no independence, but only interdependence.

But though Reverence for Life inculcates in ethical man a tremendously deep concern for the welfare, material and spiritual, of all those with whom life brings him directly or indirectly into contact, it does not therewith seek to intrude into the private sanctum of another's soul. Inquisitiveness is in fact the opposite of reverence. Only what another voluntarily chooses to reveal of himself to his friend is common property between them.

"No one should try to force his way into the personality of another . . . for there is a modesty of the soul which we must recognize, just as we do that of the body. The soul too has its clothing of which we must not deprive it, and no one has a right to say to another: 'Because we belong to one another as we do, I have the right to know all your thoughts.' Not even a mother may treat her child in that way."

Our lives indeed interpenetrate and are interpenetrated by the lives of others; yet each has its own inviolable sanctuary. At the core of the being of each one of us is a shrine which no other can enter; and a name which none knoweth save he that receiveth it.

"None of us can truly assert that he really knows someone else, even if he has lived with him for years. Of that which constitutes our inner life we can impart, even to those most intimate with us, only fragments; the whole of it we cannot give, nor would they be able to comprehend it. We wander through life together in a semi-darkness in which none of us can distinguish exactly the features of his neighbor; only from time to time, through some experience that we have of our companion, or through some remark that he passes, he stands for a moment close to us, as though illumined by a flash of lightning. Then we see him as he really is. After that we again walk on together in the darkness, perhaps for a long time, and try in vain to make out our fellow-traveller's features . . .

"In this matter, giving is the only valuable process; it is only giving that stimulates. Impart as much as you can of your spiritual being to those who are on the road with you, and accept as something precious what comes back to you from them . . .

"Much sorrow, pain, and mutual estrangement come from people claiming the right to read the souls of others, as they might a book that belonged to them, and from wishing to know and understand where they ought simply to believe. We must beware of reproaching those we love with want of confidence in us if they are not always ready to let us look into all the corners of their heart.

"We might almost say that the better we get to know each other, the more mystery we see in each other. Only those who respect the personality of others can be of real use to them . . .

"The one essential thing is that we strive to have light in ourselves. Our strivings will be recognized by others, and when people have light in themselves it will shine out from them. Then we get to know each other as we walk together in the darkness, without needing to pass our hands over each other's faces, or to intrude into each other's hearts."

Thus through reflection, through sympathy, and through service, the primary instinct of the will-to-live expands in ever-widening circles from individuality to personality, from Self to Other and simultaneously to the Source and Goal of universal Life. As man identifies himself with the experiences of other finite lives around him and participates in their joys and sufferings and efforts, he becomes increasingly aware of the presence and inspiration of an all-encompassing and indwelling Power—of Infinite Being—of "the Beyond which is also the Within." From his existence in the finite and the temporal he passes to an experience of the infinite and the eternal, from Life to Love; and this is the mystical experience. It finds its perfect consummation in union with the first-fruits and forerunner of our race who came not to be ministered unto but to minister; who came that we might have Life and have it more abundantly; who became like us that we might become like him. At the roots of our humanity lie the promise and the potency of our union with the divine. "The essential element in Christianity as it was preached by Jesus and as it is comprehended in thought, is this: that it is only through Love that we can attain to communion with God. All living knowledge of God rests upon this foundation; that we experience Him in our lives as Will-to-Love . . . Love is the spiritual beam of light which reaches us from the Infinite."

S Seaver

GEORGE SEAVER was born in 1890. For five years he was a Native Commissioner in Northern Rhodesia. Subsequently he was ordained in the ministry and for several years was a lecturer in moral philosophy. In 1944 he published his first study on Dr. Schweitzer, *Albert Schweitzer: Christian Revolutionary.* This was followed by *Albert Schweitzer: The Man and His Mind* (1947) and *Albert Schweitzer: A Vindication* (1949). He is now Dean of Ossory and Rector of Kilkenny and Canon of St. Patrick's Cathedral, Dublin, Ireland.

ALBERT SCHWEITZER,
HUMANITARIAN

▶

by EVERETT SKILLINGS

SINCE early childhood Albert Schweitzer has been deeply troubled by the vast amount of suffering in the world. In his beautiful book, *Memoirs of Childhood and Youth*, he tells us that as far back as he can remember, he was saddened by the amount of misery he saw around him. When a boy, the sight of an old limping horse, pulled forward by a man while another kept beating it with a stick, haunted him for weeks. Furthermore, he could not understand why, in his evening prayers, he should pray only for human beings. So when his mother had prayed with him and said good-night, he used to add silently a prayer he had composed for all living creatures; it ran thus, "O Heavenly Father, protect and bless all things that have breath, guard them from all evil, and let them sleep in peace."

Similar experiences moved him to a conviction that we have no right to inflict suffering on any living creature unless there is an unavoidable necessity for it.

When young Schweitzer was twenty-one, it came to him on a bright summer morning, as he awoke in his home, that he must not accept the happiness of his boyhood as a matter of course: "Proceeding to think the matter out at once with calm deliberation, while the birds were singing outside, I settled with myself before I got up, that I would consider myself justified in living for science and art until I was thirty, in order to devote myself from then onward to the direct service of humanity."

At first his thoughts were directed toward work in Europe with abandoned orphaned children or with tramps and discharged prisoners. Then one evening in the autumn of 1904, he picked up a magazine of the Paris Missionary Society which someone had placed on his desk. Skimming through it, his eye caught the title of an article entitled, "The Needs of the Congo Mission." The article captured his imagination. "My search was over; I quietly began my evening's work."

And so for nearly seven years Schweitzer studied medicine and surgery at Strasbourg University. Strenuous years they were, for he had to earn his living while preparing to become a jungle doctor. On Sundays he preached; and during the week he taught a class of theological students. Besides, there were numerous concert trips to make. He wrote a book of more than 800 pages on the music of Johann Sebastian Bach; an essay on Organ Building; and the final chapter of his *Quest of the Historical Jesus.*

While Schweitzer was preparing to become a doctor, his fiancée, Helene Bresslau, daughter of Prof. Bresslau, the eminent Strasbourg historian, was in training to become a nurse. They were married on June 18, 1912. He has frequently paid tribute to her share in his healing ministry to the African blacks. She is of the same heroic mould as he. He gratefully recognized his indebtedness to her by dedicating his book *Civilization and Ethics*: "To my Wife, the Truest of Comrades."

On Good Friday, 1913, the Schweitzers left their Alsatian home in Günsbach on the long journey to the jungles of Africa. Dr. Schweitzer took along a zinc-lined piano, built especially for the tropics—a gift of the Paris Bach Society. It had a pedal attachment, so that he might keep up his organ playing. "At first," he said, "I did not have the heart to practice. I had accustomed myself to think that this activity in Africa meant the end of my life as an artist. One evening, however, as I was playing one of the Bach organ fugues, the idea came suddenly to me that I might, after all, use my free time for the very purpose of perfecting my technique."

Their destination was Lambaréné on the Ogowe river in French Equatorial Africa, in the Trader Horn region, about forty miles from the equator. It is interesting to learn that an American medical missionary, Dr. Robert H. Nassau, established the mission at Lambaréné in 1876. Great was the joy of the aged founder, when Dr. Schweitzer sent him the news that Lambaréné was once more supplied with a doctor.

The Ogowe region has a hot, humid climate with little range of temperature. During the rainy season, torrid heat prevails, with the nights as hot as the days. Here live the remnants of eight once-powerful tribes where for three centuries the slave trade and rum had wrought havoc. Sleeping-sickness, swamp-fever, and many tropical ailments—such as malaria, leprosy, dysentery, and ulcers—occur. Pneumonia and heart disease are very prevalent. But cancer and appendicitis are fortunately unknown.

From the very first days at Lambaréné, before Schweitzer even had time to unpack his drugs and instruments, he was besieged by sick people.

In the summer of 1915, he was summoned to visit the sick wife of another missionary 160 miles upstream. Lost in thought he sat on deck, struggling to find the conception of the ethical, which he had sought but not found in any philosophy. Sheet after sheet he covered with disconnected sentences, merely to keep his mind concentrated on the problem. Late on the third day, at the very moment when at sunset they were making their way through a herd of hippopotamuses, there flashed upon his mind, unforeseen and unsought, the phrase, Reverence for Life.

"The iron door had yielded; the path in the thicket had become visible. Now I had found my way to the idea which, if put into practice, might save civilization." For several weeks after this discovery, Dr. Schweitzer lived, he tells us, in a condition of perpetual excitement. "Now there stood out clearly before my mind the plan of my whole philosophy. What Christianity needs is that it be filled to overflowing with the spirit of Jesus." In going thus to one of the worst climates in the world, in order to cure African Negroes, Albert Schweitzer proved that his deeds eloquently supplement his words.

"A heavy guilt rests upon our civilization," says Schweitzer. "What have the white peoples not done to the colored people since the era of discovery? We must serve them. When we do good to them, it is not benevolence—it is atonement."

"It is true," Schweitzer says, "that the life I see around me presents the dreadful spectacle of life struggling for its own existence at the expense of other life. Yet within me, a human being, there exists this mysterious urge to save life." In short, to preserve life is good; to destroy life is evil. At this point, Albert Schweitzer is a pioneer. The great fault of all ethics has been that it was thought to deal only with the relation of man to man; but a person is ethical only when all life as such is sacred to him—that of other animals and plants as well as man.

There is nothing of the fantastic in Schweitzer's nature. He is an eminently sane person, as all are aware who come in contact with him. He confesses that he is obliged to become a persecutor of the little mouse which infects his dwelling and is a wholesale murderer of the bacteria which may endanger his life.

How then does Dr. Schweitzer's attitude differ from that of a utilitarian? Schweitzer answers: in the first place, before destroying life, one must be very sure of the necessity; and in the second place, there must be no complacency. One must never become callous and unfeeling about taking life and causing suffering, even when it is necessary. "The good conscience," says Schweitzer, "is an invention of the devil."

Albert Schweitzer believes that the profoundest truths are not attainable through the process of reasoning, but rather that truth is attained as an immediate experience through love and intuition. The great danger for all mysticism is that of being without ethical interests. There is always the possibility that the mystic will experience the eternal as absolute impassivity, and will in consequence cease to regard action, which ethics implies, as the highest manifestation of spirituality.

Ethics implies action—putting into practice the words of Jesus: "If you know these things, happy are you if you do them." (John 13:17).

In Schweitzer's book, *Civilization and Ethics,* he discusses fully the two streams of ethical philosophy—Egoism and Altruism. He calls them self-fulfillment and self-dedication. He says: St. Paul has merged them in I Corinthians, Chapter 13, in the description of the attributes of the Love-Principles.

Everett Skillings.

EVERETT SKILLINGS was born in Portland, Maine, in 1873. He studied at Bates College, Harvard, Berlin, and Oxford He taught at Middlebury College and now is professor emeritus. He first met Dr. Schweitzer in Europe in 1932 He was one of the founders of the Albert Schweitzer Fellowship and served as secretary-treasurer from 1939 to 1948 and as president in 1949. He is author of the "Postscript, 1932-49" of the current American editions of *Out of My Life and Thought.* He now lives at Peake Island, Maine.

AN EMISSARY
OF WESTERN
CIVILIZATION

▶

by ADLAI E. STEVENSON

IT IS difficult for any person to describe adequately the role and impact of Albert Schweitzer as a world citizen.

A large part of this impact arises from the fact that Dr. Schweitzer has devoted a lifetime to the pursuit of universals that know no national or continental limits: knowledge, truth, beauty, and spirit of compassion for fellow man.

But perhaps his greatest contribution as a world citizen lies not in his pursuit of these universals but in his role as an emissary of Western civilization.

To those of us who are part of it, Western civilization means an unprecedented freedom and material well-being for the individual. Unhappily, this is not the universal view of Western civilization. Many non-Western countries look upon us as a force striving to alter their established pattern of living in order to feed our industrial machines with raw materials. Too often, we have not exported the best in our civilization—our heritage of freedom and knowledge.

This is what Dr. Schweitzer has done, by devoting his life to spreading and sharing the medical achievements of Western science, the artistic achievements of Western music, and the compassion of Christianity.

Dr. Schweitzer has shown by his example how great a force for good a single human being can be. There could be no greater fulfillment of the role of "world citizen."

Adlai E. Stevenson

ADLAI E. STEVENSON was born in Los Angeles, California, in 1900. He was educated at Princeton University and Northwestern University. He was admitted to the Illinois Bar in 1926 and was assistant to the Secretary of the Navy from 1941-44. He was governor of the State of Illinois from 1948-52. Among his books are *Major Campaign Speeches* (1952), and *Call to Greatness* (1954). He was Democratic Presidential Candidate in 1952 and now lives in Half Day, Illinois, a suburb of Chicago. He was present at a civic luncheon honoring Dr. Schweitzer in Chicago in 1949.

THE ANSWER
OF ALBERT SCHWEITZER
TO THE SEARCH FOR
THE HISTORICAL JESUS

▶

by MARTIN WERNER

AS A theologian, Albert Schweitzer is probably known to contemporary theologians best of all through his great work, *The Quest of the Historical Jesus*. In the extensive theological literature of the turn of our century, there are only a few works which could appropriately be re-edited in the decades following the first world war. Schweitzer's *Quest of the Historical Jesus* belongs to the small number of theological writings which have lost nothing of their pertinence in spite of the developments in recent thought.

What maintains the vitality of the interest in this book? For one thing, there is no other theological work which gives such comprehensive information concerning all the problems of the historicity of the person of Jesus, problems which were discovered in the last two hundred years, ever since one began to try and answer these questions. Furthermore, the presentation is so alive from the first to the last page, and so illuminating and honest in its objectivity, that the history of the problem, from the age of enlightenment to the twentieth century, confronts the reader with dramatic intensity and movement. I still remember how I first discovered the book in the library of the New Testament seminar of the University of Tübingen. It was in the summer of 1913, when I was a fifth semester student. After reading the first pages, I found that the book did not release its hold on me. I had to finish it in one sitting.

Finally, the book has a special significance because of the original solution to the problem developed by Schweitzer himself. This solution has been received by many theologians with astonishment and feelings of estrangement, not only when it first appeared (1906), but also today, when it often evokes a similar reaction. This is so because Schweitzer's picture of the historical Jesus has little to do with the figure of Christ as handed down by traditional church dogma. The theology of the enlightenment in western Christianity has made men realize that the oldest gospels present Jesus neither as the second person of the divine trinity nor as the incarnated divinity in whom two totally different "natures" are combined, one entirely human, another entirely divine. This fact has been recognized for a long time and has never since been completely forgotten.

The true historical Jesus, according to Schweitzer, is different not only from the Christ of church doctrine, but he does not correspond either to the modernized picture drawn by the gospel commentary of present-day Protestant theology. The conception of Schweitzer is striking in two respects. On the one hand, he concludes that our knowledge of the historical Jesus is more extensive and certain than modern theology dared assume in its exposition of the gospel accounts. He assures us: "The eschatological interpretation of the life of Jesus terminates all doubt of the reliability of the gospels of Mark and Matthew. It shows that their account of the public activities and of the death of Jesus follows a true tradition, accurate even in its detail." His second discovery is that the most significant difficulties in the quest for the historical Jesus do not lie in the area of historical perception, but are rather of a religious nature. Historical knowledge makes us conscious of the fact that Jesus did not announce religious truths "in a form totally divorced from all temporal significance, to be simply accepted by all generations of man." We mean by eschatological interpretation that his religion of love appears within the framework of the expectation of the end of the world of late Judaic religion. This is a pattern of thought which we can no longer accept as such. For that reason we must transpose it into terms pertinent to the modern *weltanschauung*.

Schweitzer proposes to theologians that it is the unconditional duty of religious truthfulness to take account of these facts. But he is far from assuming that Christian piety itself can be destroyed by such truthfulness, since it is the nature of piety to be determined not by philosophical conceptions of the world, but by the "will" it expresses. Schweitzer says with great insistence: "The true understanding of Jesus is the understanding of his 'will' by our 'will.' The true relationship to him is the state of being deeply affected by him. All Christian piety is valuable to him only in so far as it expresses devotion of our will to his will." That is why Schweitzer's *Quest of the Historical Jesus* finishes with the words: "He comes to us as One unknown, without a name, as of old, by the lake-side, He came to those men who knew Him not. He speaks to us the same word: 'Follow thou me!' and sets us to the tasks which He has to fulfill for our time. He commands. And to those who obey Him, whether they be wise or simple, He will reveal Himself in the toils, the conflicts, the sufferings which they pass through in His fellowship, and, as an ineffable mystery, they shall learn in their own experience Who He is."

The paradox of the striking effectiveness of Schweitzer's conception is that the picture he draws of the historical Jesus, in its unaccustomed uniqueness, seems so improbable to some theologians, even though or rather because Schweitzer bases it so definitely on the historical reliability and credibility of the older gospels. Schweitzer, eighty years old today, is just as convinced of this credibility as he was fifty years ago, when he came to his conviction in his intensive studies at Strasbourg. However, from the start he had to fight the suspicion that his trust in the historical reliability of the earlier gospels was based on an uncritically "naive attitude toward these accounts." Ever since the gospel criticism of David Friedrich Strauss and Bruno Bauer, there has been repeated evidence of sceptical suspicion—often on the part of the wider public— that the gospel accounts are historically unreliable. One must not forget that only a few decades ago people were still violently debating, "Did Jesus live?" The question was attracting world-wide attention. Even for contemporary theology, the problem of the historicity of the gospel accounts frequently presents considerable difficulties. This often finds expression in the dogmatic assertion that the gospels were not even supposed to be understood as historical accounts, but as testimonies in which their authors strongly reaffirmed their Christian faith. Thus it is quite understandable that modern man in general, and lay historians today in particular, not infrequently adopt a sceptical approach and believe that whatever historical nucleus is contained in the gospel accounts of Jesus is partly or entirely hidden behind the uncontrollable formation of legend.

Scepticism is, however, in no way a reliable test of true critical perspicacity. On the contrary, the turn to scepticism denotes the breakdown of critical approach and thus fails to solve the problem at hand. Whoever profoundly studies the problems of the research concerning the life of Jesus will be readily convinced that Schweitzer confidently accepts the historicity of the early gospels not because he judges these things more naively than the sceptics, but because his criticism sees through the real problems with greater insight than they do.

It is important to note in this connection that Schweitzer's *Quest of the Historical Jesus* accords considerable space precisely to those scholars who were most critical of the reliability of the gospel accounts. This applies, for instance, to David Friedrich Strauss, Bruno Bauer, and to the modern critics of the historical existence of Jesus. Here Schweitzer reaches the following fundamental conclusion: everyone who contests the historicity of Jesus takes upon himself the task of explaining, adequately and scientifically, and without abandoning the assumption that Jesus did not live, the origin of all the gospel accounts, of the other New Testament books, and of Christianity itself. In *The Quest of the Historical Jesus*, Schweitzer notes that past research shows the insuperable difficulties of such an undertaking. They appear "invincible and unsurmountable." Since Schweitzer said this, research has discovered nothing to contradict his conclusion and it is completely improbable that it will do so in the future. It is true that this argument does not prove the historicity of the gospel tradition. It shows, nevertheless, that the task of finding a positive solution to the problem is scientifically meaningful. It is instructive to observe how critically and methodically Schweitzer reached his confident conclusion concerning the historical reliability of the older gospels.

The gospel investigations of the nineteenth century were intent on establishing valid conclusions concerning the reliability of the different gospels by comparing them with each other. In his method of evaluating these attempts, Schweitzer once again manifests his critical judgment. Today, half a century after the composition of *The Quest of the Historical Jesus,* he needs to retract none of his essential conclusions. Schweitzer takes the following position toward the two types of gospel tradition—which modern theology also recognizes—the synoptic tradition represented by the first three gospels and the Johannine position of the fourth; the gospel of John must be rejected on principle as a source for the life of Jesus, primarily because its theological content represents the hellenistic Christianity of the era subsequent to the apostles. This estimate is valid and is not affected by the various hypotheses as to who wrote the gospel of John or when it was composed—before or after the turn of the first century—and whether the Johannine indications concerning the life of Jesus can be reconciled with those of the synoptic tradition. In the gospels of Mark and Matthew, the synoptic tradition appears in an older form than in Luke. The fact that the oldest gospel tradition can be recognized in Mark and Matthew does not in itself furnish the proof of the historicity of these gospels. On the contrary, when we begin to study this older tradition, we have only reached the position from which we can evaluate the historicity of these sources. What we decide here concerning their credibility determines whether or not we can have reliable knowledge of the historical figure of Jesus.

On what basis can one make this decision, since results cannot be controlled by comparison with other traditions? Impressed by various difficulties, previous theologians felt obligated to distinguish in the gospels what is historical and what is not. Even so, they were unable to shed definitive light on the search for an objective historical criterion which would lend a solid basis to this distinction. Schweitzer, as one of the most uncompromising theological critics, pointed to this insufficiency, realizing that absolutely everything depended on the solution of this problem and that only completely honest insight, as objective as possible, could be of help.

A special problem was posited by the accounts of miracles of the older tradition, accounts which cause understandable distrust from the very start. Schweitzer is not satisfied with pledging the theological historian most urgently to a critical attitude. He assumes the ideal of historical vision which understands the personality and the public activity of Jesus, and can explain why the account of a miracle—if it is pure invention—came to be and what historical facts were later mistakenly interpreted as miracles. As an example of striking explanations of this type, which become clear to Schweitzer with the aid of his critical method, I mention the synoptic account of the miraculous feeding of the multitude, which leads him to the surprising statement: "Everything is historical here, except the concluding remark that they were all physically satisfied."

How does Schweitzer master the dominating and fundamental search for the objective historical criterion? First of all, he establishes an important fact—based on the two oldest gospels—and thus places the problem into true perspective. He fully agrees with the common judgment that the older synoptic tradition is too fragmentary to constitute a source for the life of Jesus, i.e., for a real biography. Of essential significance for him, however, is the observation that the older gospel accounts intend to describe only the events and the history of the public activity of Jesus. In so doing, they unintentionally tell the reader that this public appearance of Jesus was of notably short duration: it took place within the span of a single year. The historian is thus concerned only with this: does he learn all that can be known about the historical figure of Jesus when he comes to understand historically, on the basis of this small number of accounts, how the mysteriously short appearance of Jesus—with its equally mysterious end—came to be in the first place, and what course it took?

In general, Schweitzer requires that any historical solution, which scientific research is to take seriously, subordinate the individual indications of the older synoptic tradition to a historical context. The historical and scientific value of any solution increases when the appreciation of such a historical context grows into complete historical understanding not only of the doctrine, activity, and fate of Jesus, but simultaneously of the origin and development of early Christianity as a whole. This value also increases as we reduce the gaps in our knowledge, which we could bridge only by tenuous hypotheses, and as we diminish the number of details in the sources which we cannot logically incorporate in any way into the context.

Like the preceding research in the life of Jesus, the analysis of the older synoptic gospels proved, however, that the establishment of an inner historic pattern of meaning was the most difficult task of all. It is true that Mark shows a general "plan" in the external sequence of the public appearances of Jesus. It extends from his meeting with John the Baptist through his activity in Galilee and a sojourn beyond the Northern frontier, to the trip to Jerusalem and to the Passion. Within this framework, however, the synoptic tradition of the older gospels appears merely as a collection of anecdotes. Inner coherences are precisely not worked out. In this connection, it becomes clear that the earlier gospel accounts, as opposed to those of Luke and John, were not consciously conceived around a theological purpose.

Here Schweitzer's penetrating critique of previous studies of the life of Jesus attained two conclusions of great importance and relevance. The first is the still undisputed proof that former attempts to arrive at a historical pattern of meaning were based on a subjective approach, on arguments not confirmed by the sources themselves. Previous scholars could, therefore, not help but proceed arbitrarily in the distinction between historical and unhistorical components of the older gospel tradition. The second conclusion is the establishment of the sole possible method for discovering the true inner coherence of these gospels. Schweitzer shows that the method consists of the attempt to clarify all indications through this single fact: in its expectation of the immediate end, the doctrine of Jesus—such as it appears in these synoptic gospels —expresses the essentially late-Judaic and apocalyptic eschatology. This most important thesis of Schweitzer has never been refuted up to the present. The radically eschatological conception of the historical Jesus, developed by him, is nothing but the clear and consequent result of his method. This was the path leading Schweitzer to his conviction that the older gospels are historically reliable; those who assert that his conviction was based on a lack of critical judgment misunderstand his entire enterprise.

It is quite true that *The Quest of the Historical Jesus* by Albert Schweitzer has lost nothing of its theological pertinence after half a century. Through this work we have gained new historical insight, which helps to bring about the long-needed reconciliation between Christian piety and the understanding of the historical Jesus. It liberates piety from encumbering errors and uncertainties.

(This essay has been translated from the German by Mr. Oscar A. Haac, Department of Romance Languages, Emory University, Georgia.)

Martin Werner

MARTIN WERNER was born in Berne, Switzerland, in 1887. From 1916-27 he was minister in the Swiss Evangelical Reformed Church Since 1928 he has been Professor of Systematic Theology at the University of Berne. He is author of *Das Weltanschauungsproblem bei Karl Barth und Albert Schweitzer* (1924) and *Albert Schweitzer und das freie Christentum* (1924).

ON THE HILL
OF ADALINANONGO

▶

by ANNA WILDIKANN

DEAR, Reverend, "Grand Docteur",
You stand before your eightieth birthday and this time I want to send you my good wishes in the form of a page of remembrance. Where shall I begin? Like visions, picture follows picture in my mind, beginning with our first meeting on that foggy November day in London, when it was impossible to see one's hand in front of one's eyes— where the world seemed at one and the same time, so narrow, and so impenetrable. Was it coincidence or was it fate, that we met that evening in the comfortable home of your old friends—the Sisters Christian? Only a few months later I came to Lambaréné.

Wherever my good wishes may go out to you at all times, on this day I cannot think of you elsewhere than at Lambaréné, on the hill of Adalinanongo, "that looks away beyond the peoples." That was how the King of the Galoas called his site there.

In my mind, as I write, is many a birthday celebration at Lambaréné. The world today knows so much about you— your achievements, your Nobel Prize; but what a birthday at Lambaréné is like, that only we who have been there, who have celebrated, and had our own birthday celebrated—know. Yours was the thought to use the birthday celebration for your co-workers in far-off Africa to replace the family circle

—the distant homeland. Was it not, too, a pedagogic thought at the end of each year of living, to take stock of the work rendered before entering on the new year?

In the morning, with the first ringing of the bell, we all stood at the door of the birthday child. You played the portable harmonium; Dr. Goldschmid, or Miss Haussknecht, the violin; and sometimes there was also a flute; and we sang two chorals—chosen by you. Do you think at times of our faithful dog Fitzko, who always accompanied us on these occasions?

After the singing we led the birthday child into the dining room. On the breakfast table there were candles burning in the red Swedish holders. A birthday cake, the traditional fried egg, and the many gifts of African rarities, or straw work, were laid at the place of the one whose birthday was being celebrated. After breakfast we all went off to work as usual: one to the operation room, the others to the hospital for the morning round, after which the examination of the sick in the polyclinic would take place. If you did not happen to be operating, you would come on the morning round of the wards, to see not only to the welfare of the patients, but also to the orderliness of the hospital. After that you would divide your time between duty in the polyclinic and in the planting of the trees, or in the construction work.

Lunch was the highlight of the day. Then it was that you made your birthday speech, and we looked forward to that moment throughout the whole year. The others know your philosophy; we in Lambaréné know your sense of humor, all the wit and all the teasing, which you—with truly French spirit—brought into these talks.

What unbelievably arresting talks you seemed to shake out of your sleeve. Unfortunately, on your own birthday you never received anything like them in return. On the contrary, mostly you had to make a speech for yourself on those occasions. I think particularly of the one which at the time touched us all so deeply. It was your seventieth birthday in January of the war year 1945. You spoke of your life and work. With deep satisfaction, you pointed out that in the seventy years of your life you had reached the fulfillment of all your wishes. Will power, contempt for idleness, and perseverance were the three principles which you had obeyed during your lifetime. You told us that your spirit was made up of three parts—one third teacher, one third pharmacist, one third peasant. By this division you left out several parts. I don't mean even the physician, but refer to the architect, for example.

Certainly your hospital is different from the modern hospitals of America and Europe. I have often been asked whether it is possible to work in those primitive buildings. I have learned to laugh inwardly at this lack of understanding. Does anyone in the world doubt the amount of work achieved at Lambaréné? Naturally, the wooden buildings with their tin roofs are not outwardly impressive. But even without air-conditioning our rooms were always cool at Lambaréné. And it strikes me that many a well-known architect would have much to learn from you. You told us how often one learns from another's mistakes, and how, in the building of your new hospital, you had changed many things which seemed unnecessary to you in other tropical constructions. Building there was certainly not easy. You had no skilled workmen to help you; and, with the undependability of the "indigenes," you were forced to supervise everything yourself, to be watchful that the doors were put in correctly, and that the latch had to be pressed down and not lifted up. I think that is something the natives will never learn. And then, the difficulties to get the tin for the roof beaten straight.

You needed it for the lining of the wooden barracks to act as a protection against fire.

That makes me think of a comic happening during my first week at Lambaréné. I did not yet know that you instructed the native workers to work in front of the pharmacy building so that a steady eye could be kept on them through the windows. Once, while I was engaged in examining a pregnant woman, their hammering—as was natural—worried me, and I asked the workmen to change their work location, and if possible, to go far away. The workmen took that as a heaven-sent excuse to stop working altogether.

Shortly after, the *Grand Docteur* appeared in my workroom, and said: "Doctor, you countermand my orders? My workers must work in front of the pharmacy. Why did you send them away?"

"Because they worried me," I replied, "and I felt they might just as well work further away. There is certainly enough space hereabout."

Whereupon you replied: "There is no need for you to think. I have already done that in anticipation."

But I did not wish to be dispensed from thinking and smouldered. That night, returning from work to my room, I found chocolate on my writing desk. That was your peace flag.

Keeping an eye on the workmen while carrying on with your own task is a typical example of your capacity for doing two things at once. I imagine that many a philosophical thought reached maturity during your supervision of the workmen or while playing your organ. Apropos the organ, where did you leave this in the division of your soul and mind into those three compartments? Well and good, your passion for organ-building I will include in the architectural section which I added. But there still remains the musician.

I would feel inclined to cancel out the pharmacist. I know you enjoy mixing ointments and that you have many chemical formulae in your head, and I like to think of those cosy evenings in Männedorf on the Zurich Lake in 1948 where I was permitted to help you in the compilation of the list of medicaments for Lambaréné. Together we studied the large books on pharmacology and the many pharmaceutical brochures. Neither of us felt inclined to interrupt our interesting task. But the intervals were even nicer, because you used them to go to the nearby church and play the organ. Mostly I accompanied you and sometimes your small grandson came too. And yet I am willing to cancel out the pharmacist; but I leave you the peasant.

Actually Lambaréné is not only a hospital, but a large farming estate. What a variety of stock and fowl there is to be found there: the smooth-haired goats and sheep, chickens and ducks, and—for the Gabon a real rarity—geese. Secretly we hoped for a roast goose, but you did not allow slaughter and so the proud geese remained the truth symbol of the hospital—just as much as the tame antelopes, monkeys, owls, parrots, and pelicans. And then the fruit orchards and the vegetable gardens—your creation! With the practical peasant approach, you gave preference to all plants which were of use. Do you remember that once I accused you of materialism? The time you wanted to fell the beautiful mimosa tree in front of my window to make room for some citrus trees? Then that evening the forester, Mr. Lau, who was visiting us, remarked on the value of the deep mimosa and acacia roots, and you turned to me and asked: "Tell me doctor, how much did you pay Mr. Lau for his plea?" I was disarmed by this suspicion, but the mimosa tree remained where it was. Actually I don't believe that I owed that to the plea of Mr. Lau, but to your own sentiment, because I appealed to it when I said: "I love this mimosa as you love your antelopes." Your antelopes that you brought up on the bottle, that shared your room, that delved with their wet noses into your pockets in search of sugar. The antelopes who chewed on your music sheets or your manuscripts or, to the great dismay of Mrs. Schweitzer, ate up the hem of your coat. We don't even wish to dwell on the evil deed of one antelope. This will be kept a secret from the world, but you, and all of us who were in Lambaréné in 1944, will never forget the danger in which it put you. *N'en parlons plus . . .*

Our estate would not be complete if we did not mention our pelicans. Our pelicans, and your pelican—*le pelican du Grand Docteur*. For you it was a question of conscience to bring up the orphaned pelicans. For me it was a hobby to photograph them, and for your pelican it was his raison d'etre to allow you to spoil him. I called him the vain and spoiled being. With what self-consciousness he would waddle along each evening to fetch his fish from you. But he was also your loyal companion. How decoratively he would perch on the ledge of your verandah door, or opposite your window at night! What a pity that pelicans are not musical! Otherwise, he might have given back to us the following morning what he had imbibed from your playing the previous night. That makes me think of Kakadu—your parrot. Do you remember how he would perch on the edge of the case holding my gramophone and whistle his part of the Mozart concerto for flute? Perhaps Moïse would not have been enthralled at this accompaniment. But we two were always pleased at how clear and true it sounded.

Now we come to the musician for whom in your assessment of your own make-up you seemed to leave no place. But no one doubts that a large part of your soul belongs there. Was not organ playing an absolute need with you even as a child? How many hours, days, and nights have you devoted to music? How much have you given to the world through your music and how many have listened to your playing? No matter how hard the day at Lambaréné had been, each and every evening you would seat yourself at your piano with organ pedals. You played for yourself or for some unseen listeners. You needed no public, but were willing, at our invitation, or to please a guest, to go up to the piano in the dining hall and play. Once, when the missionary family, O. de C., was with us and the three-year-old Noëlle could not sleep, you called her to the piano and said: "Now my child I will play a cradle song just for you and then you will go to sleep." You played, you improvised, and the child watched your fingers with those large fairy-tale eyes of hers. I stood and listened, too, but with sorrow that I was unable to note and keep this composition. Why is it that no one ever wrote down your compositions?

But your day did not end with organ playing. You wrote late into the night. Your cat—Sisi la Parisienne—lay curled up on your table; Tschuh-Tschuh, your dog, slept in front of the door; the antelopes chewed on their fodder. The crickets began to be still after having tried to drown the sound of your playing in their chirping. Other noises of the never-still tropical nights made themselves heard. That was the musical accompaniment which gave you peace for your writings.

And then—much later—when you had put away your papers, you would make a last round of the hospital. You looked at those who had undergone recent operations, at the seriously-ill patients, and also to see whether all the fires around the barracks had been extinguished. It was the last round of the doctor; but also of the watchman, who felt responsible for all those entrusted to him.

Through long years of experience, you knew how undependable the natives were—those big children, unaware of danger. You had to make sure that one of the newly-operated patients did not take it into his head to bathe in the river by moonlight; to make sure that the family of a seriously-ill patient did not take it into their heads to take him away in a *pirogue* to bring him to the witch doctor. Fortunately it did not happen often that the witch doctors interfered with our work. But one had to be on the lookout because the superstitions and the rites of the still primitive natives of the Gabon often led them on unhealing roads. From you at Lambaréné I learned to respect those rites; we were never allowed to force patients to do anything against their beliefs. That is how we learned reverence for life. This idea helped us to withstand being shut off in the jungle during the long war years.

My thoughts always go back to Lambaréné—to Lambaréné—to Adalinanongo—"that looks away beyond the peoples." But now it is that way that the peoples look . . .

Anna Wildikann.

ANNA WILDIKANN was born in Riga, Latvia, in 1902. She was educated at universities in Riga, Jena, and Heidelberg. For several years she was associated with a hospital in Zurich. She has edited, with the help of Dr. Schweitzer, two small photographic books. *The Hospital in the Jungle,* and *Doctor Schweitzer's Pelican.* Since 1950 she has been associated with the health service of Hadassah in Jerusalem, Israel. In 1934 she met Dr. Schweitzer, prepared herself to work with him, and first went to Lambaréné to be a member of his medical staff in 1937. She returned to Africa at the beginning of the Second World War and remained there until 1946 when she had to leave for reasons of health.

HOMAGE

▶

by PABLO CASALS

ON THE occasion of the celebration of the eightieth birthday of my great friend—and of the friend of all men—Dr. Albert Schweitzer, I am sending him from all my heart, my most sincere, my most cordial felicitations. I hope to be able to congratulate him anew on the occasion of his ninetieth birthday which I pray he may reach for the benefit of the great humanitarian ideas of which he is the example and the symbol.

—Pablo Casals
Prades, France.

▶

by JAWAHARLAL NEHRU

THAT Albert Schweitzer will be eighty . . . is certainly an occasion to be remembered and celebrated. I should like to express my deep admiration for the great work done by this fine man and to wish him many happy returns of the day.

—Jawaharlal Nehru
New Delhi, India.

Recent Writings

The Problem of Ethics

in the Evolution

▶

I N THE space of a single lecture I can give only a very
summary account of the problem of ethics in the evolution
of human thought. I shall therefore confine myself to the
broad outlines of that evolution, and in doing so shall attempt to make them as clear as possible.

What we call "ethics" and "morality," in terms borrowed
respectively from Greek and Latin, may broadly be said to
be concerned with the problem of how to behave well towards ourselves and towards others. We feel obliged to think,
not only of our own well-being, but of that of other people,
and of society in general.

The first stage in the development of ethics began with
the idea that this "thinking of others" should be put on an
ever-broader basis. Primitive man thinks of others only within the narrowest limits. He confines himself to those whom
he sees as distantly related to himself by blood: the members
of his tribe, that is to say, whom he regards as constituents
of the same large family. I speak from experience in this. My
patients at Lambaréné illustrate the point. Sometimes I ask
a savage of that sort to render certain little services to a
fellow-patient who cannot look after himself. He will at once
ask whether the other man is a member of his tribe. And if
the answer is "No," he will frankly reply: "This not brother
for me." Neither persuasion nor threats will induce him to

* Delivered by Dr. Schweitzer to the Académie des Sciences Morales et Poli-
tiques on his installation as a member on October 20, 1952 at the Institut
de France.

commit the unimaginable action and put himself out for a stranger. It is I who have to give in.

But as men think more and more about themselves, and about their behavior to others, they come to realize that other men, as such, are their kith and their kin. And slowly, with the evolution of ethics, they see the circle of their responsibilities grow wider and wider until it includes every human being with whom they have any sort of association.

It is on this level of understanding that we find the Chinese thinkers: Lao Tse, born in 604 B.C.; Kung Tsu (Confucius), 551-479 B.C.; Meng Tsu, 372-289 B.C.; Chuang Tsu, in the fourth century B.C.; and the Hebrew prophets Amos, Hosea, Isaiah in the eighth century B.C. The idea that we each of us have a responsibility towards every other human being was put forward by Jesus and St. Paul and is an integral part of Christian ethics.

For the great thinkers of India, be they Brahmans, or Buddhists, or Hindus, the idea of the universal brotherhood of man is part of the metaphysical idea of existence. But it is not easy for them to incorporate it in their ethical systems —for the existence of castes, in India, has erected barriers between man and man which have been sanctified by tradition and cannot now be abolished.

Nor, in the seventh century B.C., could Zoroaster encompass the notion of the brotherhood of man. He had to distinguish between those who believed in Ormuzd, the god of goodness and light, and the unbelievers, who remained under the aegis of the demons. He insisted that the believers, in their struggle to bring about the reign of Ormuzd, should consider the unbelievers as their enemies and treat them accordingly. To understand the situation, we must remember that the believers were Bactrian tribesmen who had adopted a sedentary mode of life and wanted to live as honest and

peaceable farmers; the unbelievers were tribes who had remained nomadic, lived in the desert, and supported themselves by pillage.

Plato, Aristotle, and the other thinkers of the classical
period of Greek philosophy thought only in terms of the
Greek—the Greek freeman, moreover, who was not concerned
to earn his own living. Those who did not belong to that
aristocracy they regarded as inferior beings and unworthy of
serious attention. Only in the second period of Greek
thought—that in which Stoicism and Epicureanism flowered
simultaneously—did both schools become willing to accept
the idea of human equality, and of the intrinsic interest of
human beings as such. The most remarkable champion of
this new conception was the Stoic, Panaetius, who lived in
the second century (180-110) B.C. It is Panaetius who is the
prophet of humanism.

The idea of the brotherhood of man never became popular
in ancient times. But there is great importance for the future
in the fact that philosophers should have acclaimed it as
eminently rational. We must admit, though, that the idea
that a human being as such has a right to our interest has
never enjoyed the full authority to which it might lay claim.
Right up to our own time it has been menaced, as it is today,
by the importance which we ascribe to differences of race, or
religious belief, or nationality. It is these differences which
make us look upon our kinsman as a stranger deserving of
indifference, if not, indeed, of contempt.

Anyone who analyzes the development of ethics must take
into account the influence which is exerted upon ethics by
the particular conception of the world to which it is related.
There is, of course, a fundamental difference between these
various conceptions. This difference lies in the particular
way of looking upon the world itself. Some thinkers believe

that we should take an affirmative view of the world—interest ourselves, that is to say, in its affairs and in the part we ourselves play in them. Others take a negative view, and advise us to take no interest at all in the world, or in our own existence within it. Of these two attitudes, the affirmative is nearer to nature; the negative view does violence to it. The one invites us to be at home in the world and to take a vigorous part in its affairs; the other urges us to live in it as strangers and to choose non-activity as the basis of our life here. Ethics, as such, belongs to the affirmative faction. It springs from the need to act; and to act for good. Consequently the affirmation of the world is favorable to the development of ethics; the negative attitude, on the other hand, must thwart that development. In the first case ethics can offer itself for what it is; in the second, it must give up the idea of doing so.

The thinkers of India deny the world. So do the Christians of antiquity and of the Middle Ages; the Chinese sages, the Hebrew prophets, Zoroaster, and the European thinkers of the Renaissance and modern times—all are champions of affirmation.

The Indian thinkers denied the world because they were convinced that true existence is immaterial, immutable, and eternal, and that the existence of the material world is artificial, deceptive, and ephemeral. The world which we like to consider real is merely, in their eyes, a mirage of the immaterial world in time and space. It is a mistake for us to interest ourselves in this phantasmagoria and in the part we play in it. Non-activity is the only form of behavior that is compatible with a knowledge of the true nature of existence. Of course non-activity has an ethical quality, in a certain degree. A man who renounces the things of this world renounces with them the egoism which material interests and vulgar covetousness would otherwise inspire in him. Moreover, non-activity implies non-violence. It saves a man from the danger of harming others by acts of violence.

Non-violence is extolled by the philosophers of Brahmanism, Sankhya, and Jainism. Like Buddha, they consider it the high-point of ethics. It is, however, imperfect and incomplete. It allows a man to be egoistic to the point of thinking of nothing but his own salvation. This he hopes to secure by a mode of life which conforms to a true knowledge of the nature of existence. It exacts this, not in the name of compassion, but in the name of a metaphysical theory; and though it asks him to abstain from evil it does not require him to act in accordance with the wish to do good.

Only an ethical system which is allied to the affirmation of the world can be natural and complete. If the Indian thinkers take it into their heads to yield to the promptings of an ethic more generous than that of ahimsa, they can do so only by making concessions to the affirmative point of view—and to the principle of activity. When Buddha takes a stand against the coldness of the Brahman doctrine and preaches the virtues of pity he can hardly resist the temptation to break free of the principle of non-activity. More than once he gives in to it and cannot help committing acts of charity or recommending his disciples to do the same. Under the cover of ethics, the affirmation of the world carries on an underground struggle, for century after century in India, against the principle of non-activity. In the Hindu religion, which is a religious reaction against the exactions of Brahmanism, this affirmation actually gets recognized as the equal of non-activity. The entente between them is proclaimed and specified in the Bhagavad-Gita, a didactic poem which is incorporated in the great epic of the Mahabharata.

The Bhagavad-Gita admits the Brahman conception of the

world. It recognizes that the material world has only a deceptive reality and cannot claim to engage our interest. It is merely, the poem says, an amusing spectacle which God has mounted for his own diversion. It is only as a spectator, therefore, that man is authorized to take part in it. But he has the right to suppose that he is to continue playing his part in the entertainment. He is justified in doing so by the fact that he knows why he is doing it. The man who goes about his work in the world with no other intention than that of doing God's will pursues the truth every bit as effectively as he who opts for non-activity. Undiscerning activity, on the other hand—activity which is prompted by interest in the world and the wish to achieve some object, however trivial—such activity is wrong and cannot be justified.

No ethic worthy of the name can be satisfied by the concept of the world as a diversion which God has put up for his amusement. True ethics asserts the necessity of action. The theory did, however, allow ethics to keep going in India at a time when its existence was threatened by Brahmanism.

Contemporary thinkers in India make great concessions to the principle of activity, and affirm that it is also to be found in the Upanishads. That is quite true. The explanation is that in ancient times, as we learn from the Veda hymns, the Aryans of India led a life that was filled with a naive delight in living. The Brahman doctrine of the denial of the world only appears alongside the doctrine of affirmation in the Upanishads—sacred texts that date from the beginning of the first millennium before Christ.

*　　*　　*

The Christianity of antiquity and the Middle Ages preaches the denial of the world but does not, as a consequence, enjoin non-activity. This peculiarity derives from the fact that its denial of the world is quite different from that preached by the Indians. Christianity declared that the world as we know it is not a phantasmagoria, but an imperfect world which is destined to be transformed into the perfect world: that of the Kingdom of God. The idea of the Kingdom of God was created by the Hebrew prophets of the eighth century B.C. It is also at the heart of the religion founded by Zoroaster in the seventh century B.C.

Jesus announced the imminent transformation of the material world into the world of the Kingdom of God. He exhorted mankind to seek that perfection which would enable it to enjoy a new existence in the new world. He preached the abandonment of the things of this world. To do good was the whole duty of man. Man was allowed, in fact, to be indifferent to the world, but not to his duty towards other men. Action keeps all its rights, in the Christian ethic, and all its obligations too. That is where it differs from the ethic of Buddha, with which it has in common the idea of compassion. Animated as it is by the spirit of activity, Christian ethics retains an affinity with the affirmation of the world.

The early Christians regarded the transformation of the world into the Kingdom of God as near at hand; but it has never occurred. Therefore during antiquity and the Middle Ages Christians despaired of this world and yet had none of those hopes which had buoyed up the early Christians. It would have been natural had they come round to the affirmation of the world. Their ethic of activity made it quite possible. But in antiquity and Middle Ages there did not exist that passionate affirmation of the world which alone would have served the purpose. This passionate affirmation came into being at the time of the Renaissance. Christianity joined forces with it during the sixteenth and seventeenth centuries.

Along with the ideal of self-perfection which it derived from Jesus, its ethics now embraced the Renaissance ideal: that of creating new and better conditions, material and spiritual alike, in which human beings could live together in society. Thenceforward Christian ethics had a specific end in view and could attain to its fullest development. The civilization in which we live, and which we now have to sustain and to perfect, was born of the union between Christianity and the enthusiastic affirmation of the world which we owe to the Renaissance. The ethical conceptions of both Zoroaster and the Chinese sages were affiliated, from the very beginning, with the affirmation of the world. They, too, carry within themselves energies which could bring forth a civilization based on ethics.

After attaining a certain level, ethics tends to develop in depth. This tendency manifests itself in the compulsive search for the fundamental principle of good. Ethics no longer finds complete satisfaction in defining, enumerating, and enjoining various virtues and various duties. It seeks to analyze the link which unites them in their diversity, and to discover how it is that they all flow from a single conception of good. It was in this way that the great Chinese sages came to proclaim goodwill towards all fellow-men as the root of virtue. Even before Jesus, Hebrew ethics concerned itself with the problem of the one great Commandment: the law which was to comprise all law. In accord with the traditions of Hebrew theology, Jesus raised love to the rank of the supreme commandment.

In the first century of the Christian era certain Stoics followed the path laid down by Panaetius, the creator of the idea of humanism. They too came to consider love as the virtue of virtues. These men were Seneca, Epictetus, and the Emperor Marcus Aurelius. Fundamentally their ethic was that of the great Chinese sages. They had in common with them not only the principle of love, but—what is really important—the conviction that it stems from reason and is fundamentally reasonable.

During the first and second centuries of our era, Greco-Roman philosophy came, therefore, to profess the same ethical ideal as Christianity. There seemed every possibility of an entente between Christianity and the ancient world. Nothing came of it. The ethics of Stoicism never became popular. Moreover the Stoics considered Christianity as the worst of superstitions. Was it not based on a "divine revelation" that had occurred in the person of Jesus Christ? Did not Christians await the miraculous coming of a new world? Christianity, for its part, despised philosophy as mere terrestrial wisdom. They were also divided by the fact that philosophy kept to the idea of the affirmation of the world, and the Christians to its denial. No agreement was possible.

And yet, centuries later, they did reach an understanding. In the sixteenth and seventeenth centuries Christianity became familiar with the passionate affirmation of the world which the Renaissance had bequeathed to European thought. It also made the acquaintance of the ethics of Stoicism, and was amazed to find that Jesus' principle of love was there put forward as one of the truths of reason. Among the thinkers who recognized their double allegiance—to Christianity and to Stoicism—were Erasmus and Hugo Grotius.

Under the influence of Christianity, philosophical ethics acquired an element of passion which it had not previously possessed. Under the influence of philosophy, Christian ethics began to reflect upon what it owed to itself and what it had to accomplish in the world. Consequently there arose a spirit which would no longer tolerate the injustice, the cruelty, and the harmful superstitions which it had previously allowed. Torture was abolished, and with it the scourge of sorcery trials. Inhuman laws gave place to others more clement. Reforms unprecedented in human history were conceived and carried out in the first excitement of the discovery that the principle of love is ordained by reason.

*   *   *

Certain eighteenth-century philosophers — among them Hartley, Baron d'Holbach, Helvétius and Bentham—thought that the argument of sheer utility was sufficient to demonstrate the rational necessity of altruism. The Chinese and the Stoics had also advanced this argument, but they had used others as well. The eighteenth-century thesis was that altruism is merely an enlightened form of egoism, and a conclusion drawn from the fact that the well-being of individuals, and of society as a whole, can only be assured by a system of mutual devotion. This superficial view was contested by Kant, among others, and by the Scottish philosopher David Hume. Kant, wishing to defend the dignity of ethics, went so far as to say that its utility should not be taken into consideration at all. Manifest as it may be, it should not, he said, be accepted as an ethical motive. The doctrine of the categorical imperative asserts that the commands of ethics are absolute. It is our conscience that reveals to us what is right and what is wrong, and we have only to obey. We carry within us a moral law which gives us the certainty of belonging not only to the world as we know it in time and space but also to the world as such—the world, that is to say, of the spirit.

Hume, on the other hand, proceeds empirically in his attack upon the utilitarian thesis. Analyzing the motives of ethics, he concludes that it is sentiment, above all, which governs them. Nature, he argues, has endowed us with the faculty of sympathy, and it is this that allows us, and in fact compels us, to enter into the joys, the apprehensions, and the sufferings of others. We are, he says, like strings that vibrate in unison with those of the orchestra. It is this sympathy which leads us to devote ourselves to others and to wish to contribute to their well-being and to that of society. Philosophy since Hume—if we leave Nietzsche out of account—has never seriously questioned that ethics is above all a matter of compassion.

But where does this leave ethics? Can it limit and define our obligations towards our fellow-men? Can it reconcile egoism and altruism, as the utilitarian theory attempted to do?

Hume barely considers the question. Nor has any later philosopher felt bound to consider the consequences of the principle of devotion-from-compassion. One might almost think that they sensed that these consequences might prove disquieting. And disquieting they are. The ethic of devotion-from-compassion no longer has the character of a law, as we should wish it to have. It no longer embodies cut-and-dried commandments. It is fundamentally subjective, and leaves to each one of us an individual responsibility of deciding to what point our devotion should go.

Not only are there no longer any precise commandments: ethics has come to concern itself less and less with what is possible (the province, after all, of all law). It is constantly obliging us to attempt what is impossible, and to extend our devotion to the point at which our very existence is compromised. In the hideous times which we have lived through, there were many such situations; and many, too, were the people who sacrificed themselves for others. Even in everyday life, and although the ethic of devotion may not demand of us this last sacrifice, it often requires us to ignore our own interests and to relinquish our advantages in favor of others. Too often, alas! we manage to stifle our conscience, and with it our sense of responsibility. There are many conflicts, moreover, in which the ethic of devotion abandons us to ourselves. How often can a great industrialist congratulate himself on having given a post, not to the man who was best qualified, but to the man who most needed it? Woe betide such people if they decide, after one or two experiments of this sort, that the argument from compassion may always be overruled.

*   *   *

One last conclusion must be drawn from the principle of devotion: it no longer allows us to concern ourselves only with other human beings. We must behave in exactly the same way towards all living creatures, of whatever kind, whose fate may in some respect be our concern. They too are our kith and our kin, inasmuch as they too crave happiness, know the meaning of fear and suffering, and dread annihilation. To a man who has kept his feelings intact, it is quite natural to have pity for all living creatures. Philosophy likewise should decide to acknowledge that our behavior towards them must be an integral part of the ethics which it teaches. The reason is quite simple. Philosophy is rightly apprehensive that this immense enlargement of the sphere of our responsibilities will deprive ethics of whatever chance it still has of framing its commandments in a reasonable and satisfying way.

The man who is concerned for the fate of all living creatures is faced with problems even more numerous and more harassing than those which confront the man whose devotion extends only to his fellow human beings. In our relations with animals and birds we are continually obliged to harm, if not actually to kill them. The peasant cannot rear all the new-born animals in his flock. He can only keep those which he can feed, and which will eventually repay what they have cost him. In many cases we have to sacrifice certain lives in order to save others. A man who rescues a strayed bird may have to kill insects or fish to keep it alive. Such actions are entirely arbitrary. What right has he to sacrifice a multitude of lives in order to save the life of a single bird? And if he kills off what he considers to be dangerous animals, in order to protect more peaceable ones—then there too he is in the realm of the arbitrary.

Each one of us, therefore, must judge whether it is really necessary for us to kill and to cause pain. We must resign ourselves to our guilt, because our guilt is forced upon us. We must seek forgiveness by letting slip no opportunity of being of use to a living creature.

How great an advance it would be if men could only remember the kindness that they owe to such creatures, and if they could refrain from harming them, through thoughtlessness! If we have any self-respect, where our civilization is concerned, we must struggle against those feelings and those traditions—and they are many—which do violence to humanity. I cannot refrain in this connection from naming two practices which should no longer be tolerated in our civilization: bull-fighting, where the bull is put to death, and stag-hunting.

Ethics is only complete when it exacts compassion towards every living thing.

*   *   *

There has been another great change in the position of ethics: it can no longer expect to be supported by a conception of the world which, in itself, justifies ethics.

In every age ethics has been supposed to conform to the

true nature of the universal will which is made manifest in Creation. It was in conformity with this will that ethics issued its commands. Not only was religion based upon this conviction; the rationalist philosophies of the seventeenth and eighteenth centuries also took it as their base.

But the ethical conception of the world is based upon its own optimistic interpretation of that world. Ethics endows the universal will with qualities and intentions which give satisfaction to its own way of feeling and judging. But during the nineteenth century, research—which after all can only be guided by regard for the truth—was compelled to admit that ethics can expect nothing and gain nothing from a true knowledge of the world. The progress of science consists in an ever-more-precise observation of the processes of nature. It is this which allows us to make use of the energies which manifest themselves in the universe. But at the same time these researches oblige us, in an ever greater degree, to relinquish all hope of understanding its intentions. The world offers us the disconcerting spectacle of the will-to-life in conflict with itself. One existence maintains itself at the expense of the other. In the world as it is we see horror mingled with magnificence, absurdity with logic, and suffering with joy.

How can the ethic of devotion be kept going without the support of a notion of the world which justifies it? It seems destined to founder in scepticism. This is not, however, the fate to which it is foredoomed. In its infancy, ethics had to appeal to a conception of the world which would satisfy it. Once it realizes that devotion is its basic principle, it becomes fully aware of its nature—and, in doing so, becomes its own master. We too, by meditating on the world, and on ourselves, can come to understand the origins and the foundation of ethics. What we lack is complete and satisfactory knowledge of the world. We are reduced to the simple observation that everything in it is life, like itself, and that all life is mystery. True knowledge of the world consists in being penetrated by the mystery of existence, and of life. The discoveries of scientific research merely make this mystery yet more mysterious. The penetration of which I speak corresponds to what the mystics call "learned ignorance"—ignorance, that is to say, which at least grasped at what is essential.

The immediate datum of our consciousness, to which we revert whenever we want to understand ourselves and our situation in the world, is this: I am life which wants to live, and all around me is life that wants to live. Myself permeated by the will-to-life, I affirm my life: not simply that I want to go on living, but that I feel my life as a mystery and a standard of value. When I think about life, I feel obliged to respect all the will-to-life around me, and to feel in it a mysterious value that is the equal of my own. The fundamental idea of good, therefore, is that it consists in preserving life, in favoring it and wishing to raise it to its highest point; and evil consists in the destruction of life, in the injury of life, or in the frustration of its development.

The principle of this veneration of life corresponds to that of love, as it has been discovered by religion and philosophy in their search for the fundamental notion of good.

The term "reverence-for-life" is broader and, for that reason, less vital than that of love, but it bears within it the same energies. This essentially philosophical notion of good has also the advantage of being more complete than that of love. Love only includes our obligations towards other beings. It does not include our obligations towards ourselves. One cannot, for instance, deduce from it the necessity of telling the truth: yet this, together with compassion, is the prime characteristic of the ethical personality. Reverence for one's own life should compel one, whatever the circumstances may be, to avoid all dissimulation and, in general, to become oneself in the deepest and noblest sense.

Through reverence-for-life we enter into a spiritual relationship with the world. Philosophy has tried, and tried in vain, to build up some grandiose system that will bring us into contact with the absolute. The absolute is so abstract in character that we cannot communicate with it. It is not given to us to put ourselves at the service of the infinite and inscrutable creative will which is at the basis of all existence. We can understand neither its nature nor its intentions. But we can be in touch with that will, in a spiritual sense, by submitting ourselves to the mystery of life and devoting ourselves to all the living creatures whom we have the opportunity and the ability to serve. An ethic which enjoins us only to concern ourselves with human beings and human society cannot have this same significance. Only a universal ethic, which embraces every living creature, can put us in touch with the Universe and with the Will which is there manifest. In the world, the will-to-life is in conflict with itself. In us—by a mystery which we do not understand—it wishes to be at peace with itself. In the world it is manifest; in us, it is revealed. It is our spiritual destiny to be other than the world. By conforming to it, we live our existence, instead of merely submitting to it. Through reverence-for-life we come to worship God in a way that is simple, profound, and alive.

The H-Bomb

▶

IN THE life I lead at Lambaréné, I get so tired and I have so much work to do that I cannot keep up my correspondence as much as I should wish, nor can I find time to write on subjects about which my advice is asked.

It is quite impossible for me to write an 800-word article for you. I am obliged to summon my last reserves of energy in order to carry out the essential work I must do each day.

I cannot even take a normal night's sleep and it is almost midnight as I write these lines to you. Please excuse my delay in replying to you.

I am, however, most anxious to give my views to you personally.

The problem of the effects of H-bomb explosions is terribly disturbing, but I do not think that a conference of scientists is what is needed to deal with it. There are too many conferences in the world today and too many decisions taken by them.

What the world should do is to listen to the warnings of individual scientists who understand this terrible problem. That is what would impress people and give them understanding and make them realize the danger in which we find ourselves.

Just look at the influence Einstein has, because of the anguish he shows in face of the atomic bomb.

It must be the scientists, who comprehend thoroughly all the issues and the dangers involved, who speak to the world,

* Written in response to a query from *The Daily Herald,* London, and published in that newspaper on April 14, 1954

141

as many as possible of them all telling humanity the truth in speeches and articles.

If they all raised their voices, each one feeling himself impelled to tell the terrible truth, they would be listened to, for then humanity would understand that the issues were grave.

If you and Alexander Haddow [the professor who has pleaded for a United Nations conference of scientists on the H-bomb] can manage to persuade them to put before mankind the thoughts by which they themselves are obsessed, then there will be some hope of stopping these horrible explosions and of bringing pressure to bear on the men who govern.

But the scientists must speak up. Only they have the authority to state that we can no longer take on ourselves the responsibility for these experiments, only they can say it.

There you have my opinion. I give it to you with anguish in my heart, anguish which holds me from day to day.

With my best wishes and in the hope that those who must advise us will make themselves heard.

Peace

▶

FOR the subject of the lecture which the award of the Nobel peace prize has imposed on me as an exceptional honor I have chosen the problem of peace as it presents itself today.

I believe that thus I am following the intention of the founder of the prize, who was preoccupied with this problem as it presented itself in his time and who looked to his foundation to carry on study and research on how to serve the cause of peace. The port of departure for my thoughts will be supplied by a survey of the situation as it exists after the two wars through which we have just come.

The statesmen who shaped the world in the negotiations consequent to each of these wars did not have a happy touch. Their aim was not to create situations which could have been the beginning of a somewhat more prosperous evolution. They were concerned above all with clinging to the consequences of victory and making them last. Even if their clear-sightedness had been faultless, they would not have been able to take it for a guide. They were forced to consider themselves executors of the will of the victorious peoples. They were not able to think of organizing the relations between races on just and agreeable bases.

All their efforts were absorbed by the need to prevent the worst exactions of the popular will of the conquerors from becoming a reality. In addition, they had to be alert to what the victors were doing among themselves in the way of

* Delivered in French on Nov 4, 1954 in Oslo, Norway, on receipt of the 1952 Nobel Peace Prize.

inevitable reciprocal concessions on the questions on which their views and their interests diverged.

What is untenable in the present situation—and the victors begin to suffer in this respect as well as the vanquished—has its real origin in the fact that people have not taken sufficient account of the reality resulting from the hand dealt by history and, hence, of what is just and useful.

The historical problem of Europe is conditioned by the fact that, in the course of past centuries, particularly in the so-called epoch of the great invasions, people from the East penetrated further and further toward the West and the Southwest and took possession of the land. Thus it came about that immigrants of later days lived side by side with the people of earlier immigrations.

A partial intermixture of these peoples has been produced in the course of the centuries. New national organizations, relatively homogeneous, formed themselves inside their new boundaries. In Western and Central Europe this evolution resulted in a situation which one may consider as definitive in its broad traits and whose processes ended during the nineteenth century.

In the East and Southeast, however, the evolution has not progressed to this stage. There it has stopped at a cohabitation of nationalities which have not become welded together. Each can claim to some degree the right to the land. One can substantiate its claim by saying its people are the oldest and most numerous occupants whilst the other can put forward its ability to enhance the value of the land.

The only practical solution was for the two elements to agree to live together, in a common political state, according to the terms of a compromise acceptable to both parties. However, this state of affairs was not reached before the second stage of the nineteenth century.

From that time, in effect, national consciousness developed more and more strongly, and this had grave consequences. This development no longer allowed the peoples to be guided by historical realities and by reason.

Thus the First World War found its origins in the conditions which prevailed in Eastern and Southeastern Europe. The new structure, created after the two wars, holds in its turn the germs of a future war.

The germs of conflict are contained in any new structure following a war which does not take account of historical facts and which does not tend to a just and objective solution of the problem in the light of these facts. Only such a solution can have any lasting guarantee.

The reality of history is trampled underfoot if in a case where two peoples have concurrent historical rights to the same country, only the rights of one are recognized. Titles which two peoples can substantiate in the contested parts of Europe for the possession of the same territory are of only relative value. Both in fact are immigrants of the historical epoch. Equally people are guilty of a historical mistake if in organizing a new state of things they fail to pay attention, in fixing frontiers, to economic realities. Such a fault is committed when a frontier is fixed in such a way that a port loses its natural hinterland or a barrier is erected between a region productive of raw materials and another specially fitted and equipped for processing them.

These processes give birth to states which are not economically viable.

The most flagrant violation of historical rights, and indeed simply of human rights, consists in taking away from certain peoples their right to the land where they live so that they are forced to change their home.

The victorious forces at the end of the Second World War

decided to impose this fate on hundreds of thousands of human beings and this under the most severe conditions—a fact by which we can measure how far they fell short of their task of accomplishing a state of affairs which would be roughly equitable and which would guarantee a prosperous outcome.

The essential character of the situation in which we find ourselves after the Second World War is that it has not been followed by any peace treaty. Only by agreements having the character of truce has the war been brought to an end. It is precisely because we are not capable of a reorganization such as could be a little satisfactory that we are obliged to content ourselves with these truces, drawn up according to the needs of the moment, and of which no one can forsee the future.

There then is the situation in which we find ourselves. And now in what terms does the problem of peace present itself to us? In an entirely new fashion, just as the war of today is different from that of other times. War sets to work means of death and destruction incomparably more effective than in the past. It is therefore a bad thing, worse than it has ever been. One could consider it in times past as an evil to which one must be resigned because it served progress, because it was of itself necessary. One could hold the opinion that, thanks to war, the people of greatest worth prevailed over the others, and thus determined the march of history.

One can give as an example the victory of Cyrus over the Babylonians, which created in the Near East a civilization superior to the one which preceded it, and the victory of Alexander the Great, which in its turn opened the way to Greek civilization from the Nile to the Indus.

But it has happened also that, conversely, a war led to the replacement of a high civilization by a lower one. For example, the Arabs, in the seventh and early eighth centuries, made themselves master of Persia, of Asia Minor, of Palestine, of North Africa, and of Spain, countries where Greco-Roman civilization formerly reigned.

It appears, then, that in the past war could work as well for progress as against it. As for modern war, it is with far less assurance that one can claim that it motivates progress. The evil of which it consists weighs far more heavily than formerly.

It is worth recalling that the generation before 1914 believed that the enormous increase in the means of waging war could be counted as a favorable factor. They reasoned that the result would be reached far more rapidly than formerly and they could expect very brief wars. This opinion was accepted without contradiction.

One could believe also that the evils caused by a future war would be relatively less because one expected progressive humanization of its methods. The starting point of this supposition was the obligations assumed by the peoples in the Geneva Convention of 1864 as the result of the efforts of the Red Cross. These mutually guaranteed the care of the wounded and the humane treatment of prisoners of war, as well as great respect toward the civilian population.

This convention obtained in effect considerable results, from which hundreds of thousands of combatants and civilians were to profit in the wars to come. But compared with all the miseries of war, added to beyond all measure by modern means of death and destruction, they are very slight. Indeed, there can be no question of humanizing war.

The theory of the short war, combined with that of the humanization of its methods, meant that at the moment when war became a reality in 1914, people did not treat it as tragically as it deserved.

They thought of it as a thunderstorm which had come to purify the political atmosphere and as an event which had come to put an end to the armaments race which was ruining the people. Certain people lightheartedly approved of war because of the profit which they expected from it. Others expressed a more serious and more noble opinion that this war would be the last, decidedly the last.

Many a brave man went to war persuaded that he was fighting for the advent of an era without war.

In this conflict, as in that of 1939, these two theories showed themselves to be completely mistaken. Battles and destruction lasting years were conducted in a most inhumane fashion. Contrary to the war of 1870, the duel was not between two isolated peoples but between two great groups of peoples and thus a great part of humanity was a victim of it and the evil was made that much worse.

Since we now know what a horrible evil war is, we must not neglect any effort to prevent its return. There is additionally an ethical reason. In the course of the last two wars we were guilty of inhuman acts which make one tremble and in a future war we would go further still. This must not be.

Let us dare to face the situation. Man has become a superman. He is a superman because he not only disposes of innate physical forces, but because he is in command, thanks to the conquests of science and technology, of latent forces in nature and because he can put them to his service.

To kill at a distance, mere man used only his own physical force as when he bent a bow and shot the arrow by a quick release of the bow. The superman, thanks to an engine made for that purpose, has arrived at the point of using energy released by the explosion of a certain mixture of chemical products. This enables him to employ a projectile much more effectively and send it a much greater distance.

The superman suffers from a fatal imperfection in his spirit. He is not elevated to that level of superhuman reason which must correspond to the possession of superhuman force. He lacks the capacity to put his enormous power to work only for reasonable and useful ends instead of to destructive and murderous ends. For this reason the conquest of science and technology becomes deadly rather than profitable.

Is it not significant that the first great discovery, that of using the force resulting from the detonation of gunpowder, was offered only as a means of killing somebody at a distance?

The conquest of the air, thanks to the internal combustion engine, marks a decisive advance for humanity. Men immediately profited from the opportunity it offered to kill and destroy from a height.

This invention made evident a consequence which previously one had refused to acknowledge; the superman, in proportion as his power grows, becomes more and more of a wretched man. So as not to expose himself completely to destruction which unfurls itself from on high, he is obliged to hide underground like the beasts of the fields. At the same time, he must resign himself to witnessing the unprecedented destruction of cultural values.

A new step was the discovery of the enormous forces released by the disintegration of the atom and by its utilization. After a certain stage was reached it had to be admitted that the destructive capacity of a bomb charged with such a power had become incalculable, and that already large-scale experiments were capable of provoking catastrophies menacing the very existence of mankind.

It is only now that all the horror of our existence rises up at us. We can no longer escape the question of the future of mankind.

But the essential fact we must surely feel in our hearts, and which we ought to have felt for a long time, is that we are becoming inhuman in proportion as we become supermen. We have tolerated the mass killing of men in war—about 20,000,000 in the Second World War—the reduction to nothing by the atomic bomb of whole towns with their inhabitants, the transformation of men into living torches by incendiary bombs.

We learn of these facts through the radio or through the newspapers, and we judge them according to whether they are a success to the group of people to which we belong or to our adversaries.

While we admitted that these deeds are the result of inhumane action, that admission is accompanied by the reflection that the fact of war condemns us to accept them. By resigning ourselves without resistance to our fate, we make ourselves guilty of inhumanity.

What is important is that we should recognize jointly that we are guilty of inhumanity. The horror of this experience should shake us out of our stupor, so that we turn our will and our hopes towards the coming of an era in which war will be no more. That will and that hope can have only one result: the attainment, by a new spirit, of that higher reason which would deter us from making deadly use of the power which is at our disposal.

The first man who had the courage to advance purely ethical arguments against war and to demand a higher reason controlled by an ethical will was the great humanist, Erasmus of Rotterdam, in his *Querela Pacis* (*The Lamentation of Peace*), which appeared in 1517. In that work he showed peace seeking a hearing.

Erasmus found few disciples on this path. It was thought unrealistic (*comme une utopie*) to expect any advantage from the point of view of peace from the assertion of a purely ethical need.

Kant shared this opinion. In his work, *On Perpetual Peace,* appearing in 1795, and in other publications in which he touches on the problem of peace, he holds that its realization will come only from an authority growing out of an international law, according to which an international court of arbitration would adjudicate in conflicts between peoples.

This authority, according to him, must be based solely on the increasing respect which in time and for purely practical motives, men will accord it as a right—inasmuch as Kant insists ceaselessly on the idea that one must not advance ethical reasons in favor of peace, but that this right must be considered as a natural outcome on the road to perfection.

He thinks that that perfection will be attained in the course of a naturally developing progress. In his opinion, "nature, that great artist," will lead men—by gentle stages, it is true, and at the end of a long time, through the march of historical events and through the misery of wars—to reach agreement on an international law guaranteeing an everlasting peace.

The plan for a United Nations with powers of arbitration was formulated for the first time with some precision by Sully, friend and minister of Henry IV. It has been dealt with in detailed fashion by the Abbé Castel of Saint-Pierre, in three works of which the most important is called *Project for Perpetual Peace Between the Christian Sovereigns.* Kant drew his knowledge of the opinions he developed, probably from an extract that Rousseau published in 1761.

Today we have at our disposal the experience of the League of Nations of Geneva and of the organization of the United Nations to judge the efficacy of international institutions. These will be able to render considerable service in putting forward their mediation in conflicts at their birth, in taking the initiative in creating common enterprises of the nations, and by other actions of this nature, according to circumstances.

One of the most important achievements of the League of Nations was the creation in 1922 of a passport with international validity for people who had become displaced as a result of war. What would have been the situation of these people if, on the initiative of Nansen, the League had not created this passport for their replacement? What after 1945 would have been the fate of displaced persons if the United Nations organization had not existed?

These two institutions, however, have not been capable of leading to a state of peace. Their efforts were fated to receive a setback because they were obliged to try them in a world in which there never existed a spirit directed toward the realization of peace. Being only juridical institutions, they were incapable of creating that spirit. The ethical spirit alone has this power. Kant deceived himself when he believed that he could do without this spirit in his peace undertaking. We must follow the road on which he did not wish to embark.

And what is more, the extremely long time on which he counted for the movement toward peace is no longer at our disposal. The wars of today are wars of annihilation. Those that he imagined were not. Decisive measures for the cause of peace must be undertaken and decisive results acquired, and that with little delay. Of that also, the spirit alone is capable.

Can the spirit do effectively what we in our great need must ask it to do?

We must not underestimate its power. For it is the spirit which is manifest throughout the history of humanity. It is the spirit which has created that humanitarianism which is the origin of all progress towards a superior form of existence. Animated by humanitarianism, we are true to ourselves and capable of creation. Animated by the opposite spirit, we are untrue to ourselves and fall prey to every error.

The power which this spirit was able to exercise was sown in the 17th and 18th centuries. It brought the peoples of Europe, where it manifested itself, out of the Middle Ages by putting an end to superstition, witch trials, torture and many other cruelties and such traditional follies. In place of the old it established the new, causing never-ending wonder in those who witnessed the change. All that we have ever possessed of true and personal civilization, and which we possess still, has its origin in that manifestation of spirit.

Later it lost its power, mainly because it has failed to find a foundation for its ethical character in that practical knowledge which resulted from scientific research. It was succeeded by a spirit which failed to see clearly the way humanity was proceeding and which lacked the same high ideals. It is to the spirit we must now devote ourselves afresh if we do not want to perish. A new miracle must be wrought, similar to the one which brought the peoples of Europe out of the Middle Ages—a miracle greater than the first.

The spirit is not dead; it lives in solitude. It has surmounted the difficult duty of living without a practical knowledge to match its ethical character. It has understood that it must base itself on nothing except the essential nature of man. The independence which it has acquired in relation to knowledge has proved to be a gain.

It is convinced that compassion, in which ethics have their roots, can only achieve full scope and depth if it is not limited to men but is extended to all living things. Alongside the old ethics, which lacked this depth and force of conviction, have come the ethics of respect for life, and this has become increasingly recognized as valid.

We venture to address ourselves again to the whole man, to his faculty of thought and of feeling, to exhort him to know himself and to be true to himself. Again we want to put our trust in the profound qualities of his nature. Our experiences confirm us in this enterprise.

In 1950, a book appeared entitled *Documents of Humanity,* edited by the professors of the University of Goettingen, who had been among the victims of the horrible mass expulsion of East Germans in 1945. The refugees described in very simple terms the help they had received in their distress from persons belonging to the enemy nations, and who, in consequence, should have been moved by hate. I have seldom been so stirred by a book as I was by this. It is capable of restoring faith in humanity to those who have lost it.

Whether peace comes or not, depends on the direction in which the mentality of individuals and therefore also of nations develops. In our age, this truth is even more valid than in the past. Erasmus, Sully, the Abbé Castel de Saint-Pierre, and the others who, in their time, concerned themselves with the coming of peace, did not have to deal with peoples but with princes. Their efforts were directed towards persuading them to establish a supranational authority possessing powers of arbitration for smoothing out difficulties which might arise among them. Kant, in his *Perpetual Peace,* was the first to envisage an age where the peoples would govern themselves, and being sovereign, would have to concern themselves with the problem of peace. This development he considered to be a progressive one. In his opinion, the peoples, more than the princes, would be disposed in favor of peace, because they were the ones who suffer all the misfortunes of war.

The time has come when governments must consider themselves the executors of the popular will. But Kant's opinion about the people's innate love of peace has not been proved. Insofar as it is the will of the great mass, the popular will has not avoided the danger of instability and the risk of being diverted by passion from the path of true reason; nor does it possess the necessary feeling of responsibility. A nationalism of the worst kind has revealed itself in the course of these two wars, and at present it can be considered as the greatest obstacle to the understanding now incipient among the peoples.

This nationalism can be counteracted only by the rebirth of a humanitarian ideal among men, making their affiliation to their country natural and inspired by a genuine ideal.

False nationalism is also seething in the countries overseas, in particular among the peoples formerly under white rule and who have recently achieved independence. They run the danger that nationalism will become their only ideal. Consequently, in several places, the peace which has existed up to now is endangered.

These peoples also will only be able to overcome their naive nationalism through a humanitarian ideal. But how is this change to come about? Only when the spirit again is strong in us and we revert to a civilization based on humanitarian ideals will it react, through our intermediary, upon these peoples. Everybody, even the semi-civilized and the primitive, is able, insofar as he is equipped with the faculty of compassion, to develop a humanitarian spirit. It exists within him like an inflammable substance which only awaits to be ignited in order to break out into flame.

A number of nations which have achieved a certain level of civilization have already come to see that peace must reign one day. In Palestine it was demonstrated for the first time by the prophet Amos in the eighth century B.C. and it survives in the Jewish and Christian religions in the hope of a Kingdom of God. It is an element in the doctrine taught by the great thinkers of China; Confucius and Lao Tse in the sixth century B.C. and Mi Tse in the fifth and Meng Tse in the fourth. It was found again in Tolstoy and other contemporary European thinkers. We were pleased to consider it a Utopia. But today the situation is such that it must become a reality again in one form or another; otherwise humanity will perish.

I know quite well that when I speak on the subject of peace, I do not contribute anything that is essentially new. My profound conviction is that the solution consists in our rejecting war for an ethical reason, because it makes us capable of inhuman crimes. Erasmus of Rotterdam, and several others after him, proclaimed this as the truth which must be followed.

The only originality which I claim for myself is that in me this truth is accompanied by the certainty, born of thought, that the spirit is—in our age—capable of creating a new mentality, an ethical mentality. Inspired by such a conviction, I proclaim this truth, in the hope that my testimony can contribute to the recognition that it has validity not only in words but in practice. More than one truth has remained totally, or for a long time, without effect simply because nobody envisaged that it could become a reality.

It is only in the degree that a peace ideal takes birth among the peoples that the institutions created for maintaining this peace can accomplish their mission in the way that we expect and hope.

Once more, we live in an age marked by the absence of peace; once more the nations feel themselves menaced by others; once more we must concede to everybody the right to defend himself with the terrible weapons now available.

It is in such a contingency that we must keep a watch for the first sign of that manifestation of spirit in which we must place our faith.

This sign cannot be anything but the beginning of an endeavor on the part of the nations to repair, to the extent possible, the wrongs which they have inflicted on each other in the course of the last war. Hundreds of thousands of prisoners and deported persons await the chance to return at last to their homes; others, condemned unjustly by a foreign power, await their acquittal; and there are many other injustices which still have to be righted.

In the name of all who work for peace, I beg the nations to take the first step on this new way. None of them will, by doing this, lose a shred of the power necessary for their self defense.

If in this way we undertake the liquidation of the last war, some degree of confidence will be established among the nations. In all undertakings, confidence is the great asset without which nothing useful can be achieved. It creates in all fields the necessary conditions for fruitful expansion. In the atmosphere of confidence thus created, we should be able to undertake a just settlement of the problems created by the two wars.

I believe that I have expressed here the thoughts and hopes of millions of people who, in our part of the world, live in fear of future war. If my words penetrate to those who live in the same fear on the other side of the curtain, may they be understood in the sense intended.

May the men who hold in their hands the destiny of the peoples scrupulously avoid anything that can aggravate the present situation and make it even more dangerous. And may they take to heart the words of the Apostle Paul: "If it be possible, as much as lieth in you, live peaceably with all men." These words apply not only to individuals, but also to nations. May they, in their efforts to maintain peace, go to the farthest limits of the possible, so that the spirit has time to develop and realize itself.

Bibliography

I. Volumes Written by Albert Schweitzer

1898

Eugene Münch. Mulhouse, Alsace: Brinkmann.

1899

Die Religionsphilosophie Kants von der Kritik der reinen Vernunft bis zur Religion Innerhalb der Grenzen der blossen Vernunft. (The Religious Philosophy of Kant from the "Critique of Pure Reason" to "Religion within the Bounds of Mere Reason.") Tübingen: J.C.B. Mohr. 325 pp.

1901

Das Abendmahl im Zusammenhang mit dem Leben Jesu und der Geschichte des Urchristentums. (The Last Supper in Connection with the Life of Jesus and the History of Early Christianity). Tübingen: J.C.B. Mohr.

Vol. I. *Das Abendmahlsproblem auf Grund der wissenschaftlichen Forschung des 19. Jahrhunderts und der historischen Berichte.* (The Problem of the Last Supper in the Light of Nineteenth-Century Scientific Research and of the Historical Documents). 62pp. 2nd ed., 1929.

Vol. II. *Das Messianitats—und Leidensgeheimnis: Eine Skizze des Lebens Jesu.* (The Secret of the Messiahship and Passion; A Sketch of the Life of Jesus). 109pp. 2nd ed., 1929.
The Mystery of the Kingdom of God; The Secret of Jesus' Messiahship and Passion, trans. by Walter Lowrie. London: A. & C. Black. 275pp. 1925. New York: Dodd, Mead. 1914. New York: Macmillan. 174pp. 1950.

1905

J. S. Bach, le musicien-poète; avec la collaboration de M. Hubert Gillot. 3 vol. Paris: Costallat. 455pp. 4th ed., 1924. Leipzig: Breitkopf & Härtel.

1906

Von Reimarus zu Wrede. (From Reimarus to Wrede). Tübingen: J. C. B. Mohr. 418pp.
The Quest of the Historical Jesus; A Critical Study of its

Progress from Reimarus to Wrede, trans. by W. Montgomery. London: A. & C. Black. 410pp. 1910. 2nd English ed., 1911. 5th ed., 1922. New York: Macmillan.

Deutsche und französische Orgelbaukunst und Orgelkunst. (The Art of Organ-Building and Organ-Playing in Germany and France). Leipzig: Breitkopf & Härtel. 51pp. 2nd ed., (Nachwort über den gegenwärtigen stand der Frage des orgelbaues, 1927), 73pp., 1927.

1908

J. S. Bach, Musicien-Poète. Leipzig: Breitkopf & Härtel. 844pp. Wiesbaden: Breitkopf & Härtel. 1952.

J. S. Bach, trans. by Ernest Newman. 2 vol. Leipzig: Breitkopf & Härtel. London: A. & C. Black. 428+500pp. 1911. New York: Macmillan. 1947.

1911

Geschichte der paulinischen Forschung von der Reformation bis auf die Gegenwart. (History of the Study of Paul from the Reformation to the Present Time). Tübingen: J. C. B. Mohr. 197pp. 2nd ed., 1933.

Paul and His Interpreters; A Critical History, trans. by W. Montgomery. London: A. & C. Black. 253pp. 1912. New York: Macmillan. 252pp. 1951.

1912

J. S. Bachs Orgelwerke. Kritisch-praktische Ausgabe. (J. S. Bach's Organ Works. Critical-Practical Edition). Zusammen mit Charles Marie Widor. New York: G. Shirmer. 4 vol., 1912-14.

1913

Geschichte der Leben-Jesu-Forschung. Neu bearbeitete und vermehrte Auflage des Werkes Von Reimarus zu Wrede. (History of Research into the Life of Christ; New Revised and Enlarged Edition of "From Reimarus to Wrede"). Tübingen: Mohr, 642pp.

Die psychiatrische Beurteilung Jesu. Darstellung und Kritik. (The Psychiatric Study of Jesus). Tubingen: J. C. B. Mohr. The title of the doctoral dissertation was *Kritik der von medizinischer Seite veröffentlichten Pathographien über Jesu.* (Criticism of the Pathographs on the subject of Jesus published from the Medical Standpoint). 46pp.

The Psychiatric Study of Jesus, trans. by Charles R. Joy. Boston: Beacon Press. 81pp. 1948.

1920

Zwischen Wasser und Urwald. (Between the Water and the Jungle). Upsala: Lindblad. 1921, Bern: Paul Haupt. 1925, Munich: C. H. Beck. 154pp.
On the Edge of the Primeval Forest, trans. by C. T. Campion. London: A. & C. Black. 180pp. 1922. New York: Macmillan. 222pp. 1948.

1923

Christianity and the Religions of the World, trans. by Johanna Powers. London: Allen & Unwin. 86pp. New York: George Doran Co. 93pp. New York: Henry Holt, 86pp. 1939.
Das Christentum und die Weltreligionen. Bern: Paul Haupt. 60pp. 1924. 2nd ed., 1928.

Kulturphilosophie I: Verfall und Wiederaufbau der Kultur. (Cultural Philosophy I: The Decay and the Restoration of Civilization). Bern: Paul Haupt. Munich. C. H. Beck. 64pp.
The Decay and the Restoration of Civilization, trans. by C. T. Campion. London: A. & C. Black. 106 pp. 2nd ed., 1932. New York: Macmillan.

Kulturphilosophie II: Kultur und Ethik. (Cultural Philosophy II: Civilization and Ethics). Bern: Paul Haupt. Munich: C. H. Beck.
Civilization and Ethics, trans. by John Naish. London: A. & C. Black. 298pp. 2nd ed., trans. by C. T. Campion. 287pp. 1929. 3rd English ed. revised by Mrs. C. E. B. Russell, 1946. New York: Macmillan.
The Philosophy of Civilization, trans. by C. T. Campion. First Amer. Ed. combined. New York: Macmillan. 347pp. 1949.

1924

Aus meiner Kindheit und Jugendzeit. (Out of My Childhood and Youth). Munich: C. H. Beck. 64pp. 2nd ed., 1925, 73pp.
Memoirs of Childhood and Youth, trans. by C. T. Campion. London: Allen & Unwin. 103pp. 1924. New York: Macmillan. 103pp. 1925.

1925

Mitteilungen aus Lambaréné. (Reports from Lambaréné). I—1924. Bern: Paul Haupt. 1925. II—1924-25. Bern: Paul Haupt. 1926. III—1925-27. Bern: Paul Haupt. 1928. Also published by C. H. Beck in Munich.

"On Goethe." Trans. by C. T. Campion. New York: Henry Holt. 8pp. 1928. Also reprinted in *Hibbert Journal.* July 1929. pp. 684-90. Also in Seaver's biography, pp. 329-34.

1929

Selbstdarstellung. (Self-Portrait). In *Die Philosophie der Gegenwart in Selbstdarstellungen,* ed. by Raymund Schmidt. Leipzig: Felix Meiner. 1929. pp. 205-48.

1930

Die Mystik des Apostels Paulus. Tubingen: J. C. B. Mohr. 407pp. *The Mysticism of Paul the Apostle,* trans. by W. Montgomery and with a prefatory note by F. C. Burkitt. London: A. & C. Black. 411pp. 1931. New York: Henry Holt. 1931.

1931

Aus meinem Leben und Denken. (Out of My Life and Thought). Leipzig: Felix Meiner. 211pp.
My Life and Thought, trans. by C. T. Campion. London: Allen & Unwin. 283pp. 1933.
Out of My Life and Thought, An Autobiography, trans. by C. T. Campion. New York: Henry Holt. 288pp. 1933. 1949, with postscript by Everett Skillings. 274pp. 1952, New York: Mentor. 213pp.

Das Urwaldspital zu Lambaréné. (The Hospital in the Primeval Forest at Lambaréné). Munich: C. H. Beck. (This is a compilation of the three volumes, *Mitteilungen aus Lambaréné*).
More from the Primeval Forest, trans. by C. T. Campion. London: A. & C. Black. 173pp. 1931.
The Forest Hospital at Lambaréné, trans. by C. T. Campion. New York: Henry Holt. 191pp. 1931.

1932

Goethe, Gedenkrede gehalten bei der Feier der 100. Wiederkehr seines Todestages in seiner Vaterstadt. (Goethe, A Speech given on the Occasion of the Celebration of the 100th Anniversary of his Death in his Native City). Munich: C. H. Beck. 51pp.
Goethe: Two Addresses, trans. by Charles R. Joy and C. T. Campion. Boston: Beacon Press. 75pp. 1948.
Goethe: Four Studies, trans. by Charles R. Joy. Boston: Beacon Press. 116pp. 1949.

Goethe: Three Addresses, trans. by C. T. Campion and Mrs.
C. E. B. Russell. London: A. & C. Black. 84pp. 1949.

1935

Die Weltanschauung der indischen Denker. (The World View
of the Indian Thinkers). Munich: C. H. Beck. 201pp.
Indian Thought and its Development, trans. by Mrs. Charles
E. B. Russell. London: Hodder & Stoughton. 272pp. 1936.
New York: Henry Holt. 1936.

1938

Afrikanische Geschichten. (African Stories). Leipzig: Felix
Meiner. 88pp. 1938. Paris: Payot. 1941.
From My African Notebook, trans. by Mrs. C. E. B. Russell.
London: Allen & Unwin. 132pp. 1938.
African Notebook, trans. by Mrs. C. E. B. Russell. New York:
Henry Holt. 144pp. 1939.

1947

Albert Schweitzer: An Anthology, ed. by Charles R. Joy. Boston:
Beacon Press. 323pp.

1948

Das Spital im Urwald. (The Hospital in the Primeval Forest).
Photographs by Anna Wildikann. Bern: P. Haupt. Munich:
C. H. Beck. 52pp.

1949

The Wit and Wisdom of Albert Schweitzer, ed. by Charles R.
Joy. Boston: Beacon Press. 104pp.

1950

Ein Pelikan erzählt aus seinem Leben. (A Pelican Tells his Life
Story). Photographs by Anna Wildikann. Hamburg: R.
Meiner. 64pp.
The Animal World of Albert Schweitzer, ed. by Charles R. Joy.
New York: Harper. Boston: Beacon Press. 207pp.

1951

Music in the Life of Albert Schweitzer, ed. by Charles R. Joy.
New York: Harper. Boston: Beacon Press. 300pp.

II. Articles Written by Albert Schweitzer Translated into English

"Our Pets at Lambaréné." *Everyland* III pp. 36-38, 88-90, 114-16, 150-151, n.d.

"The Relations of the White and Coloured Races." *Contemporary Review.* January 1928. pp. 65-70. (This is also reprinted in the appendix to Seaver's biography).

"Sunday at Lambaréné." *Christian Century.* March 18, 1931. pp. 373-76. (This is also reprinted in the *Spectator,* April 4, 1931, pp. 540-41).

"Busy Days in Lambaréné." *Christian Century.* March 14, 1934. pp. 355-57.

"Forgiveness." (A Sermon). *Christian World.* November 1, 1934. p. 11.

"Religion in Modern Civilization." *Christian Century.* November 21, 28, 1934. pp. 1483-84, 1519-21. (This is also reprinted in the appendix to Seaver's biography).

"Reverence for Life." *The Animals' Magazine.* October 1935. pp. 3-4.

(Letter) *Spectator.* Sept. 6, 1935. pp. 357.

"Philosophy and the Movement for the Protection of Animals." *Int. Journal of Animal Protection.* Edinburgh. May 1936.

"The Ethics of Reverence for Life." *Christendom.* Winter 1936. pp. 225-39.

"Letter from Lambaréné." *The Living Age.* September 1938. pp. 70-72.

(Letter) *Christian Century.* March 21, 1945. pp. 380-81.

(Letter) *Christian Century.* May 30, 1945. pp. 655.

"At Lambaréné in Wartime (1939-45)." London: British Council for Dr. Schweitzer's Hospital. 1946. New York: Albert Schweitzer Fellowship. 19pp. 1947.

"The Tornado and the Spirit." (A Sermon). *Christian Register.* Sept. 1947. p. 328.

"The State of Civilization." (An Interview). *Christian Register.* September 1947. pp. 320-23.

"Our Task in Colonial Africa." In *The Africa of Albert Schweitzer,* by Joy and Arnold. 1948.

"Childhood Recollections of Old Colmar." In *Albert Schweitzer: An Introduction*, by Jacques Feschotte. 1954. pp. 107-113. This is a speech given at a reception in his honor by the municipality of Colmar on February 23, 1949.

"Your Second Job." (Ed. by Fulton Oursler). *Readers Digest.* October 1949. 6pp.

"Reconstructing the Bach Violin Bow." (Trans. by E. Niesberger). *Musical America.* July 1950.

"The Conception of the Kingdom of God in the Transformation of Eschatology." In *The Theology of Albert Schweitzer for Christian Enquirers*, by E. N. Mozley. 1950. pp. 80-108.

"I Am One of You." *Rotarian.* March 1952.

"The Problem of Ethics in the Evolution of Human Thought." In *Albert Schweitzer: An Introduction*, by Jacques Feschotte. 1954. pp. 114-30. (An imperfect translation also appears in *The Saturday Review.* June 13, 1953, pp. 9-12ff.).

"The Hospital as it is Today." *Episcopal Churchnews.* February 21, 1954.

(Foreword). In *Documents of Humanity*, ed. by K. O. Kurth. New York: Harper and Bros. 1954. pp. 9-10.

"The H-Bomb." *London Daily Herald.* April 14, 1954. (This is also reprinted in *The Saturday Review*, July 17, 1954, p. 23, and *Scientific Monthly*, Oct. 1954, p. 208.).

"Peace." *The New York Times.* Nov. 5, 1954. This is a translation of the lecture in French given in Oslo on November 4, 1954 on his receipt of the 1952 Nobel Peace Prize. (Text incomplete in all editions). *Peace News*, London. Nov. 12, 1954, pp. 2-3, (complete text).

III. Books About Albert Schweitzer in English

The World of Albert Schweitzer, by Erica Anderson and Eugene Exman. New York: Harper. 144pp. 1955.

Albert Schweitzer: Philosopher, Theologian, Musician, Doctor; Some Biographical Notes, by C. T. Campion. London: A. & C. Black. 31pp. 1928.

Albert Schweitzer—An Introduction, by Jacques Feschotte. London: A. & C. Black. 130pp. 1954. Boston: Beacon Press.

Albert Schweitzer; Genius in the Jungle, by Joseph Gollomb. New York: Vanguard. 249pp. 1949. London: P. Nevill. 1951.

Prophet in the Wilderness; the Story of Albert Schweitzer, by Herman Hagehorn. New York: Macmillan. 221pp. 1947.

The Africa of Albert Schweitzer, by Charles R. Joy and Melvin Arnold. New York: Harper and Bros. Boston: Beacon Press. 160pp. 1948.

Albert Schweitzer: His Work and His Philosophy, by Oskar Kraus, trans. by E. G. McCalman. London: A. & C. Black. 75pp. 1944.

The Theology of Albert Schweitzer for Christian Enquirers, by E. N. Mozley. London: A. & C. Black. 108pp. 1950. New York: Macmillan. 1951.

The Challenge of Schweitzer, by John Middleton Murry. London: Jason. 133pp. 1948.

Albert Schweitzer: Life and Message, by Magnus C. Ratter. London: Allenson. 260 pp. 1935. 2nd ed., 1950. 214 pp. London: Lindsey Press. Boston: Beacon Press.

Albert Schweitzer: The Man and His Work, by John D. Regester. New York: Abingdon. 145pp. 1931.

The Albert Schweitzer Jubilee Book, ed. by A. A. Roback. Cambridge: Sci-Art. 508pp. 1945.

My Monkey Friends, by Mrs. Charles E. B. Russell. London: A. & C. Black. 1938.

The Path to Reconstruction; a Brief Introduction to Albert Schweitzer's Philosophy of Civilization, by Mrs. Charles E. B. Russell. London: A. &. C. Black. 68pp. 1941. New York: Henry Holt. 1941.

Albert Schweitzer: Christian Revolutionary, by George Seaver. London: Clarke. New York: Harper. 112pp. 1944.

Albert Schweitzer: *The Man and His Mind,* by George Seaver. London: A. & C. Black. 346 pp. 1947. 4th ed., 1951. 346 pp. New York: Harper and Bros. 1947.

Albert Schweitzer: *A Vindication, being a Reply to the Challenge of Schweitzer, by John Middleton Murry,* by George Seaver. London: J. Clarke. 1950. Boston: Beacon Press. 120pp. 1951.

IV. Articles About Albert Schweitzer in English

"Schweitzer as Missionary," by W. Montgomery. *Hibbert Journal.* July 1914. pp. 871-85.

"Albert Schweitzer, Missionary, Musician, Physician," by O. Pfister. *Living Age.* Aug. 2, 1924. pp. 229-33.

"Philosophy of Civilization," by A. G. Hogg. *Int. Review of Missions.* January, April 1925. pp. 45-58, 237-51.

"Schweitzer's Ethic," by W. Montgomery. *Hibbert Journal.* July 1925. pp. 695-708.

"Can Schweitzer Save Us from Russell?" by Reinhold Niebuhr. *Christian Century.* Sept. 3, 1925. pp. 1093-95.

"Dr. Albert Schweitzer," by J. G. Tasker. *London Quarterly Review.* July 1927. pp. 106-109.

"Dr. Albert Schweitzer as Theologian," by E. Barthel. *Hibbert Journal.* July 1928. pp. 720-35.

"Interpreter of Jesus and of Bach," by J. S. Bixler. *Christian Century.* Nov. 15, 1928. pp. 1395-96.

"Dr. Albert Schweitzer's Work in Lambaréné," by J. G. Tasker. *London Quarterly Review.* January 1929. pp. 98-101.

"Why A Genius Went to the Jungle," by C. H. Moehlman. *World Tomorrow.* Oct. 30, 1930. pp. 418-19.

"One of the World's Greatest Living Men," by Hubert W. Peet. *Christian Herald.* March 1931. pp. 10-11ff.

"Philosophy in Action," by D. E. Trueblood. *Christian Century.* April 29, 1931. pp. 575-77.

"Schweitzer, His Black Brother's Keeper." *Literary Digest.* March 21, 1931. pp. 18-19.

"Albert Schweitzer's Mission to Africa," by Asbury Smith. *Christian Advocate.* July 9, 1931. Cen. Ed., pp. 679-80.

"Among the Human Leopards." *Literary Digest.* Sept. 26, 1931. pp. 18-19.

"Albert Schweitzer." In *What I Owe to Christ,* by C. F. Andrews. London: Hodder & Stoughton. 1932. Chap. XIII.

"Albert Schweitzer, Physician, Philosopher, and Musician," by Margaret Deneke. *Christian Advocate.* April 27, 1933. Cen. Ed., pp. 392-93.

"Dr. Schweitzer's Autobiography," by B. A. Barber. *London Quarterly Review.* July 1933. pp. 395-401.

"Oganga of the Africa Forest," by Hubert W. Peet. *World Outlook.* July 1933, pp. 12ff. August 1933, pp. 14ff.

"Albert Schweitzer, Christian Superman." *World Unity Magazine.* Vol. 13, pp. 89-97. 1933.

"Albert Schweitzer," by O. Heuschele. *Lutheran Church Quarterly.* January 1935. pp. 29-34.

"On Indian Thought and Development," by L. M. Russell. *Hibbert Journal.* July 1935. pp. 630-34.

"A Day with Albert Schweitzer," by Mildred Davis Skillings. *German-American Review.* September 1935. pp. 33-35, 52.

"Letter From Lambaréné." *Living Age.* Sept. 1938. pp. 70ff.

"Baffled Kindness," by B. T. Clausen. *Christian Century.* Sept. 27, 1939. pp. 1166-67.

"Schweitzer." In *Three Trumpets Sound: Kagawa, Gandhi, Schweitzer,* by Allan A. Hunter. New York: Association Press. 1939. pp. 107-50.

"A Portrait of an Internationalist," by J. S. Bixler. *Christendom.* Vol. 9, No. 1. 1944. pp. 35-39.

"Albert Schweitzer: His Work and His Philosophy," by V. Turner. *Dublin Review.* July 1944. pp. 62-69.

"Albert Schweitzer," by G. Seaver. *Spectator.* Jan. 12, 1945. p. 31.

"Kierkegaard and Schweitzer, an Essay in Comparison and Contrast," by E. M. Dodd. *London Quarterly Review.* April 1945. pp. 148-53.

"God's Eager Fool," by J. A. O'Brien. *Readers Digest.* March 1946. pp. 43-47.

"Great Man in the Jungle." *Time.* April 1, 1946. p. 66.

"Visit to Albert Schweitzer," by D. Walther. *Contemporary Review.* September 1946. pp. 160-66.

"Come and Follow Me . . ." *Time.* December 15, 1947. pp. 53-54.

"The Greatest Soul in Christendom," by Melvin Arnold. *Christian Register.* Sept. 1947. pp. 324-27ff.

"Schweitzer: Man of Action," by Emory Ross. *Christian Century.* Jan. 7, 1948. pp. 9-11.

"Albert Schweitzer," by F. Kendon. *Fortnightly.* January 1948. pp. 59-64.

"With Schweitzer in Africa," by Helene Schweitzer. *Christian Century.* April 21, 1948. pp. 345-46.

"Schweitzer's Jesus of History," by S. M. Gilmour. *Religion in Life.* Vol. 18, No. 3, pp. 427-33. 1949.

"Schweitzer Returns," by Cecil Northcott. *Spectator*. February 18, 1949. pp. 213.

"Goethe's Message and Schweitzer's," by E. H. Zeydel. *Christian Register*. June 1949. pp. 14-16.

"Schweitzer's Jungle Hospital," by Gloria Coolidge. *Christian Register*. June 1949. pp. 17ff.

"Albert Schweitzer," by W. K. Gottstein. *American Medical Association Journal*. July 9, 1949.

"Reverence for Life." *Time*. July 11, 1949. pp. 68-70.

"Greatest Christian." *Newsweek*. July 11, 1949. p. 58.

"Talk with Albert Schweitzer," by Harvey Breit. *New York Times Book Review*. July 17, 1949. p. 15-16.

"Albert Schweitzer," by Winthrop Sargeant. *Life*. July 25, 1949. pp. 74-80.

"Schweitzer at Aspen," by Allan A. Hunter. *Christian Century*. July 27, 1949. pp. 890-91.

"Goethe and Schweitzer." *Christian Century*. July 20, 1949. pp. 862-63.

"I Am The Life That Wills to Life . . ." by Hans Martin. *Christian Register*. August 1949. pp. 15-16.

"Schweitzer: Man of God," by Emory Ross. *Christian Century*. Aug. 3, 1949. p. 916.

"The Greatest Soul in Christendom and His Stand on Free Religion," by Robert H. Schacht, Jr. *Christian Register*. August, September 1949. pp. 17-19, 17ff.

"Albert Schweitzer: Humanitarian," by Raymond P. Sloan. *Modern Hospital*. September 1949. pp. 59-64.

"Schweitzer, the Philosopher," by M. Fischer. *Commonweal*. December 9, 1949. p. 271.

"Portrait . . . Albert Schweitzer," by Emory Ross. *American Scholar*. Winter 1949-50. pp. 83-88.

"The Missionary as Social Reformer: Albert Schweitzer." In *Personalities in Social Reform,* by G. Bromley Oxnam. New York: Abingdon-Cokesbury. 1950. pp. 145-72.

"Schweitzer: Philosopher in the Jungle," by J. A. O'Brien. *Catholic World*. January 1950. pp. 290-91.

"Albert Schweitzer: A Portrait Drawn for his Seventy-Fifth Birthday," by Friedrich Tillmann. *Ecumenical Review*. Winter 1950. pp. 170-75.

"Albert Schweitzer was My Teacher," by L. C. Lawson. *Etude*. December 1950. p. 13.

"Schweitzer vs. Stalin," by Harold Stassen. *Ladies Home Journal.* July 1951. pp. 36-37ff.

"Schweitzer at Günsbach," by Barnard S. Redmont. *Christian Register.* Nov. 1951. pp. 13-16.

"Schweitzer at 77," by A. Daniel. *New York Times Magazine.* January 13, 1952. p. 17.

"Albert Schweitzer, the Great Men's Greatest Man," by K. Van Hoek. *Rotarian.* March 1952. pp. 6-8.

"Apotheosis of Albert Schweitzer," by M. W. Hess. *Catholic World.* March 1952. pp. 425-29.

"With Schweitzer in Africa," by Homer A. Jack. *Christian Century.* July 16, 1952. pp. 823-25.

"Dr. Schweitzer of Lambaréné," by Douglas V. Steere. *The Friend.* Seventh Month 24, 1952. pp. 22-25.

"With Schweitzer in Africa," by Homer A. Jack. *The Progressive.* August 1952. pp. 13-14.

"A Visit with Albert Schweitzer," by Anita Daniel. *Glamour.* December 1952. pp. 82ff.

"God's Own Man," by Eugene Exman. *United Nations World.* December 1952. pp. 29-34.

"My Visit to Lambaréné," by J. Witherspoon. *United Nations World.* December 1952. p. 35.

"Schweitzer Returns," by David Hebb. *Saturday Review.* Dec. 27, 1952. p. 52.

"Schweitzer and Radhakrishnan: A Comparison," by C. W. M. Gell. *Hibbert Journal.* April, July 1953. pp. 234-41, 355-65.

"With Schweitzer in Lambaréné," by Homer A. Jack. *Saturday Review.* May 2, 1953. pp. 16-17. (Reprinted in *Saturday Review Reader No. 3.* New York: Bantam Books. 1954).

"Death at Lambaréné," by Douglas V. Steere. *Saturday Review.* June 13, 1953.

"Visit to the Africa of Dr. Albert Schweitzer," by C. Urquhart. *Phylon.* Sept. 1953. pp. 295-301.

"I Know the World's Greatest Man," by Marion Mill Preminger. *American Weekly.* January 10, 1954. p. 2.

"The Settlement of 45 Roofs," by Helen Yast. *Hospitals.* May 1954. pp. 80-82.

"Albert Schweitzer: A Picture Story of the 20th Century's Greatest Man," by Erica Anderson and Thomas B. Morgan. *Look.* June 15, 1954. pp. 34-44.

"A Pilgrimage," by Charl Ormand Williams. *National Parent-*

Teacher. June 1954. pp. 14-17.

"Visit to Albert Schweitzer," by John Gunther. *Readers Digest.* August 1954. pp. 43-48.

"Point About Schweitzer," by Norman Cousins. *Saturday Review.* Oct. 2, 1954. pp. 22-23.

"A Man of Mercy," by W. Eugene Smith. *Life.* November 15, 1954. pp. 161-72.

"Toccata and Fugue," by Joseph Wechsberg. *New Yorker.* Nov. 20, 1954. pp. 79-103.

A CHRONOLOGICAL

BIOGRAPHY

▶

January 14, 1875—Born at Kaysersberg, Alsace.

1880-84—Student in the village school at Günsbach, Alsace, where his father was pastor.

1885-93—Student at the gymnasium at Mulhouse, Alsace.

October 1893—Studied organ with Widor in Paris.

November 1893—Began studies at the University of Strasbourg.

April 1894-April 1895—Military service.

1895—Twentieth Year

Summer 1896—Resolved to devote life to the direct service of humanity beginning at the age of thirty.

1898—Published first book, a tribute to former organ teacher, Eugene Munch.

1898-99—Studied at the Sorbonne and also studied organ again with Widor.

April-July 1899—Studied philosophy and organ in Berlin.

July 1899—Received doctorate degree in philosophy at Strasbourg.

December 1899—Appointed to the staff of St. Nicholas church in Strasbourg.

December 1899—Book on Kant published.

July 1900—Obtained a licentiate degree in theology.

September 1900—Ordained at St. Nicholas as a regular curate.

May 1901—Provisional appointment at St. Thomas Theological School in Strasbourg.

1901—Book on the Last Supper published.

October 1903—Appointed principal of St. Thomas College in Strasbourg.

1905—Thirtieth Year

January 14, 1905—Informed friends of decision (to study medicine and go to Africa) and began study of medicine at Strasbourg.

1905—Biography of Bach published in Paris.

1906—Books on Jesus and on organ-building and organ-playing published.

1908—German edition of biography of Bach published.

1911—Book on Paul published.

June 1912—Married Miss Helene Bresslau.

1912—First of four volumes of his edition of Bach's works published.

February 1913—Received degree of doctor of medicine, after having finished thesis and completed a year of interneship.

March 26, 1913—Embarked at Bordeaux for the first sojourn in Africa, building hospital near Lambaréné, Gabon, French Equatorial Africa.

1913—Thesis on the psychiatric study of Jesus published and second edition of his book on Jesus also appeared.

1914—Interned at Lambaréné as an enemy alien (German national).

1915—Fortieth Year

September 1915—Concept of reverence for life "discovered" while journeying on Ogowe River.

September 1917—Taken to France with wife and interned.

July 1918—Returned to Alsace in an exchange of internees.

1919-21—Accepted pastorate at St. Nicholas in Strasbourg and also became a hospital physician.

January 14, 1919—Only child, Rhena, born.

1920—Honorary doctorate from theological faculty in Zurich.

1920-24—Gave lectures and organ concerts in many European countries.

1923—First two volumes of his philosophy of civilization published.

April 1924—Second sojourn in Africa and moved hospital to new site also near Lambaréné.

1925—Fiftieth Year

July 1927—In Europe for lectures and concerts.

August 28, 1928—Received Goethe Prize from the City of Frankfort.

December 1929—Third sojourn in Africa.

1930—Second book on Paul published.

1931—*Out of My Life and Thought* published.

February 1932—In Europe for lectures, concerts, and writing.

April 1933—Fourth sojourn in Africa.

February 1934—In Europe and later gave Hibbert Lectures at Oxford and Gifford Lectures at Edinburgh.

1935—Sixtieth Year

1935—Book on Indian thought published.

February 1935—Fifth sojourn in Africa.

September 1935—In Europe to give concerts, deliver second course of Gifford Lectures, and to make organ recordings.

February 1937—Sixth sojourn in Africa.

February 1939—Arrived in Europe and returned to Africa on next boat because of the possibility of outbreak of Second World War.

March 1939—Seventh sojourn in Africa.

1945—Seventieth Year

October 1948—In Europe for first time since beginning of Second World War.

July 1949—First trip to the United States.

October 1949—Eighth sojourn in Africa.

June 1951—In Europe to visit Mrs. Schweitzer and to give concerts and lectures.

1951—Elected to membership in French Academy.

December 1951—Ninth sojourn in Africa.

July 1952—In Europe to lecture and give recitals.

October 1952—Delivered lecture to the French Academy.

December 1952—Tenth sojourn in Africa.

1952-53—Three 12-inch long-playing records of Bach issued.

November 1953—Awarded the 1952 Nobel Peace Prize.

June 1954—In Europe.

November 1954—Delivered speech in Oslo, Norway, on presentation of Nobel Prize.

1955—Eightieth Year

January 14—Celebrated 80th birthday.

ACKNOWLEDGEMENTS

▶

T HE editor of this *Festschrift* has never had an easier task or more willing collaborators.

He is indebted to all who have contributed to this volume.

He is grateful to those with whom he initially consulted about the compilation of this collection: Mr. Melvin Arnold, Mrs. Julian Rogers, and Dr. Emory Ross. He has also received valuable suggestions from Prof. James L. Adams and Prof. Paul A. Schilpp. He is thankful to the translators for rendering four of these essays into English: Miss Phyllis Fisher, Dr. Maurice S. Friedman, Mr. Oscar A. Haac, and Dr. Felix Pollak. He is obligated to *The Saturday Review* for allowing the use of the essay by Mr. Norman Cousins (which was originally promised for this collection) and to the Abingdon Press for allowing the reprinting, with changes, of the essay by Bishop G. Bromley Oxnam from his *Personalities in Social Reform*.

The editor, as publisher, is grateful to those persons who have purchased copies of this Festschrift and thus have made possible its publication.

Most of all, the editor is indebted to Dr. Albert Schweitzer for allowing him to visit Lambaréné and Günsbach. At both places he caught something of the spirit of *Le Grand Docteur* and also was introduced to that dedicated circle of the friends and co-workers of Albert Schweitzer.

H.A.J.

1405 Chicago Avenue
Evanston, Illinois
December 1, 1954